D0114529

Only Golf Spoken Here

ONLY GOLF SPOKEN HERE

❖ BY IVAN MORRIS ❖

C0LOURFUL MEMOIRS

of a

PASSIONATE IRISH GOLFER

Sleeping Bear Press

Sleeping Bear Press
310 North Main Street
P.O. Box 20
Chelsea, MI 48118
www.sleepingbearpress.com

Printed and bound in Canada.

10 9 8 7 6 5 4 3 2 1

Library of Congress Cataloging-in-Publication Data

Morris, Ivan, 1945-
  Only golf spoken here / by Ivan Morris.
    p. cm.
ISBN 1-58536-052-X
1. Golf—Ireland—Anecdotes. 2. Morris, Ivan, 1945-
3. Golfers—Ireland—Biography. I. Title.
GV967 .M72 2001
796.352'092—dc21

00-012294

This book is dedicated to my wife, Marie, who has never been jealous of the love affair I openly and brazenly carried on for so many years with a mistress named golf, and to my late father, Tom, who, in spite of his famous golfing name, played off a modest sixteen handicap for most of his long golfing career. Dad always encouraged and supported me in everything I tried to do in my life, and I know he would approve of this book.

Acknowledgments

I wish to acknowledge and thank the following people. First of all, the late Charles E. Anderson of Portmarnock and County Sligo Golf Clubs. In 1986, Charles published a pamphlet called "A Personal Account of Golfing Experiences, 1926–1986." He kindly gave me a copy. I was so enamoured with Charles's reminiscences that I promised myself that as soon as I started looking back at my own golfing life rather than looking forward, I would write my own memoir.

It was my wife, Marie, who decided when this would be. In January of 1999, I must have been getting on her nerves because, out of the blue, she ordered me to start writing.

"Just get on with it!" she ordered, as only a wife can do.

Before I had gone too far, I spoke to Tony Finn of Cork Golf Club. Tony had written and self-published a hilarious fictional spoof, *Through the Green Lightly*, which is based on imaginary (or are they?) characters in the legendary Irish golfing village of Lahinch. He explained the mechanics of writing and publishing and everything he told me was "spot on."

I showed the first, crude draft to one of my best golf buddies, Sten Mathews, who, like me, has been an enthusiastic and voracious reader of golf material all of his life. He was my first critic. Between the "buts," "ifs," and "maybes," he seemed to be giving me the green light.

Then I requested the advice of a trusted family friend who claimed he knew "practically nothing" about golf, P.J. McAuliffe. He hemmed and hawed and said, "You put golf on a pedestal, don't you? Do not be afraid to knock it off (the pedestal). You are too serious. Let your sense of humour show through!"

In times gone by, that comment might have brought about a swift punch on the nose. But I knew he was right and I have done my best to follow his sound advice.

In the meantime, I was receiving nothing but the fullest support from my family. My brothers, Robert, Brien, and Dermot, all made their contributions. My mother, who was the inspiration for the title, was sent back fifty years in time to help me with my spelling and grammar.

Then a golf therapist, Veronica Conlon, came into my office to order some printing. I asked her if she would read my work and tell me if the psychological stuff I had in it would stand up to professional scrutiny. She was most enthusiastic. Veronica introduced me to John deGarmo. John is an advertising man who has been heavily involved in the production of several golf books. John really wound me up, changing my attitude completely and inspiring me to think commercially.

I networked unsuccessfully for about six months trying to find a publisher. My friend Pete Trenham in Philadelphia asked the author James Finegan, whose golf books I have very much enjoyed myself, if he could offer any help. Finegan told me about Sleeping Bear Press in Michigan. Bingo! That was the last piece of the jigsaw.

When the renowned professional writer, Lorne Rubenstein, said he was prepared to spend his valuable time reading an early draft and give it a generous endorsement, it was hugely encouraging and personally flattering.

Thank you all most sincerely.

Everybody has a story to tell; everybody has a book in them. This is my story. In lots of ways I have led a charmed life and I am grateful for it. Of course there have been disappointments along the way, but golf, like life, is not perfect. I was a slow learner. It took me longer than it should have to realise that golf is only a game and should be played for pleasure, while always recognising that the greatest enjoyment comes from playing well.

I have plucked up the courage to write down some of my memories and experiences of a game that has treated me with outrageous fortune, both good and bad. I have to say that looking back I was enjoying myself more than the impression I sometimes gave, but trying hard and giving my all was of the essence to me.

I hope the reader will be amused by my tales and touched by the passion I have felt toward the game right from the first time I had the pleasure of creaming one straight down the middle. My cousin, the late Roland Stafford, a one-time touring professional and a first-class musician, told me once, "Just because you know all the notes does not mean you can play like Paderewski." How right he was! But I had to find that out for myself, the hard way.

TABLE OF CONTENTS

Foreword

By Lorne Rubenstein

Welcome to Ivan Morris's delightful ramble through his golf-saturated life, which is still only in the middle of the back nine. Here you will find his keen insights into Irish and world golf, for Ivan is nothing if not a seriously obsessed and talented golfer who also appreciates the written word. He also has a gift for the spoken word, and he must have written down every golf conversation he ever had, if one is to judge by the details contained in this memoir.

Now, I happen to have been a longtime fan of Irish golf, and have traveled frequently to points north and south there. The way we met was unusual, to say the least. Suffice it to say that I was taken aback after he introduced himself to me during the 1991 Irish Open, and there in the press center opened his briefcase, pushed a button on a tape recorder, and what came out but my voice! He had been mysteriously acquiring taped copies of a program I broadcast on Canadian TV and wanted to discuss its merits or otherwise. I should have run from Ivan there and then. Instead we developed a friendship that has stayed the course of a decade. The man is a certified golf nut. Thankfully, he studies the game and knows his stuff. And his opinions!

Well, read them for yourself and laugh and weep.

There's more to Ivan than golf, however. Really. You will, incidentally, find out his views on many aspects of life here. He is an inspector of life with an eye for detail. Ivan is also a family man, whose wife Marie is a saint. Believe me. This is one hospitable woman. Some years ago my wife Nell and I spent an enjoyable day in their Limerick home. Ivan watched golf on television while also discoursing on Irish politics during commercial breaks. Marie showed Nell her beautiful garden, and not a word about golf passed between them. Outrageous, but this was a necessary balance to what was occurring inside as Ivan showed me every golf magazine he had and discussed more nuances of the swing than the teachers he admires ever considered. We then moved on to discuss the approach to the 11th green at Ballybunion, the merits of kick points on shafts, the heaving glories of Royal County Down, and the sublime pleasures of Lahinch.

These subjects, and more, Ivan covers with brash and bright words. You are in for a treat. Take up residence in your favorite armchair, with a glass of Guinness or of good Irish whiskey (there is no bad Irish whiskey) and fall under Ivan's spell. But be careful. Should you write to tell him how much you enjoy the book—and it's highly likely that you will enjoy it—then it's possible you will find yourself with a new lifelong friend.

Then again, that's not such a bad thing, is it?

⊛
CHAPTER I

I Have Been to Heaven
An unforgettable trip to Augusta

"Well gentlemen, they really got down to the dirt today!"

So said Jack Nicklaus, halfway leader of the 1981 Masters Tournament at Augusta, when he came into the Media Center after his second round. The double meaning was intended. Several players suffered the indignity of putting off greens. Hal Sutton, the reigning U.S. Amateur  Champion, was on the back of the par-five fifteenth green in two shots and putted right off the front into the water, recording a seven. Others putted off the ninth green and watched the ball roll thirty or forty yards back down the fairway. Ben Crenshaw turned his back to the hole at the sixteenth and found a boomerang-like route into the can. From a distance of twenty feet, his ball must have travelled forty. You have seen this stuff on TV often enough to know that I am not hallucinating. Nor is it any exaggeration to say, all of these years later, that while the world's best players suffered on "greens from hell," I watched, and thought I was in heaven.

The 1981 Masters was not the best ever, but it had its moments. Tom Watson won by just edging ahead of Jack Nicklaus and a youthful Greg Norman, playing in his first Masters. When the decisive shot was played at the seventy-first hole, I was in the thick of it, standing only a few yards away from the future Captain of Ballybunion Golf Club (Watson) when he played the decisive bunker shot that sealed victory. I was stunned by the speed at which Watson sized up and played that famous shot. He had an air of destiny and confidence about him that was unforgettable. I bumped into Tom, quite by chance, at Lahinch in 1999 and asked him about his matter-of-fact approach to that bunker shot. He merely shrugged and said it was a very straightforward shot. I told him that it was easy for him to say that eighteen years later! But what was I doing at the Masters Tournament anyway, and how did I get such sought-after tickets?

1980 was probably my most successful season playing golf, in spite of the fact that my wife, Marie, went through a terrible time giving birth to our son, David, in May of that year. While Marie struggled and was in and out of hospital, I won an Irish Senior Cup medal, the Inter-provincial Championship, the European Clubs' Championship (Kas Trophy), the Castletroy Scratch Cup, the Captain's Prize at Ballybunion, and the President's Prize at Limerick Golf Club. I promised Marie a really good holiday in 1981 to make up for all the suffering and discomfort that David and I had put her through. In the fall of 1980 we went to a family wedding, where we met Marie's Uncle Dick and Auntie Maureen (Phelan) from Waterford. To our amazement they told us that their daughter Mary, Marie's first cousin, and her husband, Dr. Conor O'Neill, were living in Augusta, Georgia, and were working in the local hospital.

"Had we ever heard of it?"

Ha! Had we ever! Right there and then I began to plot. I had not been to America since 1966 when I was a student, and Marie had resisted the idea of a trip to the United States until then, but the thought of going to Augusta in

In May 1980 David's birth was brought forward so that his father could play in the Interprovincial Championships at Royal County Down. All turned out well for mother and baby, and the championship was won! David was comfortable lodged in a cup which met a fiery demise a year later when the City of Derry GC clubhouse was destroyed by an IRA bomb. Left to right: Ivan, Caroline, David and Marie.

April to see all the beautiful flowers for which Augusta is famous was easy to sell. Marie also genuinely enjoyed watching golf, which was just as well, being married to me. We contacted the O'Neills to find out if they had a spare bed available. In fact, it did not matter if they had or had not; we were coming anyway, and would sleep on the floor, if necessary. Conor and Mary had been living in Augusta for two years, and though they were not golfers they had managed to get to the tournament the previous year and were smitten by it. They were well aware of how difficult tickets were to come by and had little or no prospect of acquiring tickets a second time. They said that we were "most wel-

The Very Reverend Canon Gerard Enright, P.P., with his housekeeper Nellie Joyce, who baked our brown soda bread and scones.

come" to come, provided we brought tickets for them, too! Things became more complicated when my golfing mentor of long standing, the late Very Reverend Canon Gerard Enright P.P., upon hearing the news that Marie and I were going to Augusta, announced straight away that he was going to come, too.

"I just have to visit the holiest golf shrine on God's earth before I am taken away to the great clubhouse in the sky," he declared. "There is no guarantee that there is golf in heaven, but there is heaven at Augusta!"

I knew my reverend friend's penchant for colourful exaggeration was off the mark on this occasion. Heaven would not be heaven at all without our favourite pastime. There was no escaping the fact that this all added up to five of us intending to go to the Masters without a single ticket in sight. My friend Pat Ruddy, the golf writer and publisher, was contacted to see what he could do. From time to time, I had written articles for Ruddy's *Golfer's Companion* maga-zine, and not wishing to infringe my amateur status, had never accepted any payment; but now it was time to look for "something" in return, in the shape of Masters tickets.

At the same time Father Enright decided to do his own networking. To his surprise he found out that the parish priest of Mary on the Hill Parish in Augusta was a Father Michael Dulea, from Macroom, County Cork. He wrote to Dulea and promptly received a reply, which went something like this:

"Glad to hear you are coming for the Masters. As it happens I could do with some extra help that week. You are very welcome to stay here in the Presbytery. I will announce from the altar a week or two ahead of the tournament that a golf-crazy priest from Ireland is coming over to assist me. God willing, we might pick up a spare ticket or two. I have never tried this before but I am sure it will work."

Father Gerry, whose faith in the power of a parish priest was much greater than mine, thought that this was eminently satisfactory and declared that we should go full speed ahead with our arrangements. Marie and I booked a holiday in Tampa, Florida, where we would visit my foster father, George Edmondson—whom I had not seen for 15 years—before travelling up to Georgia. Father Gerry went to the east side of Florida to watch Raymond Floyd win the Tournament Players Championship at the brand new (and highly controversial) Sawgrass Golf Club. We arranged to meet at Augusta in due course. No tickets had arrived before we departed, but Ruddy told me "not to worry" and to present myself to the Pinkerton Security men at the gate and ask for one Charley Yates, who would take care of everything. Yates was a friend and contemporary of Bobby Jones. Both were members of East Lake Country Club, in Atlanta. He had enjoyed a great career in amateur golf himself, playing on the U.S. Walker Cup team and winning the 1938 British Amateur Championship by defeating an Irishman, Cecil Ewing from Sligo, in the final.

I arrived at the course on the Monday before the tournament, still without a ticket. I showed my press identifi-

cation to the man on gate duty. He arranged to have me
escorted up Magnolia Lane, on foot, to the office. Yates was
not there, nor were any tickets. Charley could not be
found. It was confirmed that he was the only one who
could give out tickets. Presumably because it was Monday,
and everything was fairly low key at that point, I was not
asked to leave, and was allowed to wander off on my own.

I went to the Media Center, with which I was familiar
from my previous visit in 1966. By a stroke of luck, I met a
friendly receptionist there, Mrs. Hazel Salmon, who knew
Father Dulea, and who said she was charmed by my brogue.
She allowed me to use her phone. I rang Ruddy in Dublin.
He said he was helpless (I could have killed him!) but he
would try to contact Joe Carr, the legendary Irish amateur
player, who was a member of the Augusta National club and
had competed in the Masters a number of times himself as
British Amateur Champion, to see if he could do "something." I was not a bit happy about this, as I had never been
very friendly with Carr. In fact, there was a mild hostility
towards him on my part because he had never seen fit to
select me to play for Ireland during his term of team cap-
taincy. I was acutely apprehensive and in no way confident
that this final throw of the dice would bear fruit, but I was
wrong. Joe, to his eternal credit, came up trumps. Somehow,
he found Yates on the end of a telephone line. Within an
hour, a message was delivered to Mrs. Salmon to tell me
that I was going to be given a full working media badge,
including entry to the clubhouse. Back to the office I went
to thank Mr. Yates and pick up the ticket. A further half an
hour was spent recounting every little anecdote I knew
about Joe Carr, Cecil Ewing, John Burke, and James Bruen,
all legendary Irish amateur golfers who had played in the
Walker Cup matches. At the same time I was fervently trying
to persuade Charley, now bubbling with good old Southern
charm, to give me a second ticket for Marie. Boy, was he
tough. You would think he was protecting a one-stroke lead
down the final hole of the tournament. In the end my per-

sistence and my stories about Irish golf wore him down and I was "allowed" to purchase one extra ticket at face value ($75). Imagine my feelings when I got back for dinner that evening, and before I could announce my good fortune I was met by a beaming Father Enright, who told me that three tickets—count 'em, three tickets—had been handed in to the Presbytery for "the Irish Priest." Now we had five tickets—enough for all of us. I should never have doubted the power of a parish priest!

All that effort and heart-in-mouth stuff was worth it, because being at Augusta is indeed like being in heaven. No amount of TV viewing could prepare you for the beauty and atmosphere of the place. One of the first things to strike home is how hilly and tiring the course is to walk. There is a drop of almost 1,000 feet from the tenth tee to the twelfth green. The magnificent tall pine trees that line the fairways are ideal for spectators to walk under while watching play and being sheltered from the hot Georgia sun. The trees are spaced so far apart on most of the holes that they do not really come into play. There was no rough, and the fairways were "miles" wide. This did not matter because Augusta is a "second shot course," calling for ultraprecise approach play in order to leave flat putts on wicked surfaces. That is the real test of Augusta: It calls for highly focused course management and planning, and avoiding three-putt greens seemed to be every bit as dominant in the players' minds in 1981 as it is nearly twenty years later. Any putting from the wrong shelf on those terraced greens was the "kiss of death" and a sure invitation to bogey. Or worse.

The speed of the greens was hugely controversial in 1981. One by one the players coming into the Media Center moaned and groaned. Even the normally sensible and objective Nicklaus whined. Almost to a man, every blow-by-blow account of the day's play was preceded by a derogatory comment about the greens. The previous year, apparently, the club had decided to change to a bentgrass type instead of the traditional and much slower "grass of the South,"

My wife, Marie, at The Masters in 1981.

Bermuda. The players were finding it difficult to make the necessary adjustments in their mental approach and putting techniques. I could not help feeling sympathy for them and thinking to myself that the course was tricked up a shade too much. Lady Luck seemed to me to be more of a factor in the final outcome than it should have been.

On Friday evening after play had ended, Marie and I were walking back through the course to the car park beside the fifth fairway when we met a friendly greenkeeper making his way onto the thirteenth green pushing a hand mower. We asked him how low the blades were on his mower. He told us between 1½ and ²⁄₁₆ of an inch, and that each green had to be mowed four times between rounds. No wonder they were so fast. The thirteenth was "his" green. This was his second mowing, and two more would follow in the morning before the early starters reached the hole. We were told the greens would be "at death's door by the end of the week, and would be unplayable, and the course closed, in two weeks from now." Nowhere on the course was there a weed in sight. Never have I seen such perfection. The tees were cut as tightly as the greens back home.

On Saturday, on our way to the course, a "gentleman" approached us. He asked if we had tickets. When we said "Yes," he offered us $1,000. I thought about it for three seconds and said, "No thanks, we could not sell our tickets to heaven. The gods of golf would not approve." We had not travelled that far and gone to so much trouble just to make a few dollars.

My favourite holes for watching the action were the third, tenth, thirteenth, and sixteenth. The third is a short, tantalising uphill par four. The second shot must be weighted absolutely perfectly. The tenth is a 485-yard par four and the thirteenth a 465-yard par five. Figure that out. Is there any other course in the world where such an anomaly exists? The descent from tee to green at number ten makes the hole play much shorter than its yardage. Watching the players having fits trying to sink putts on this wickedly pitched green provided me with hours of entertainment. At No. 13, the severe bend to the left puts a limit on the distance one can drive a straight ball. A controlled quick hook is needed. Rae's Creek on the left makes that strategy fraught with danger. At No. 16, a par four, there is an air of magical expectancy. So often it has been the pivotal hole in deciding the eventual winner. Twos and sixes are recorded as regularly as clockwork. The green slopes diabolically from right to left towards the water, and there is sand all the way along the right-hand side. It is a hole that you cannot play safely. You must play it aggressively, sometimes with disastrous consequences. Above all, it is a marvellous amphitheatre. You have to get down there early if you want prime viewing.

The clubhouse is a very modest structure. Inside, it is more functional than elegant. The colour green is prominent everywhere. Green carpets. Green napkins. Waiters with green vests gliding about. The food is surprisingly simple and inexpensive. I could not help thinking how great it would be to be the Champion just once, if only to stun the members of that exclusive club by ordering a pre-tournament meal of the traditional Limerick kind. For starters I'd have Packet and Tripe, used to build up the power and strength of our rugby players. This, by the way, is the lining of a sheep's stomach boiled in milk and onions. For the main course, Corned Beef and Colcannon (a mixture of mashed potatoes, onions and pickled cabbage) would do nicely.

To be able to sit near the putting green outside the colonial style clubhouse with a cooling drink and watch the whole world of golf go by is an experience to savour. Where else could you see so many world-renowned players of the past and present in the same place? Legislators, media, celebrities and captains of the golf industry—all together doing business and enjoying themselves. In the middle of all of these VIPs every year is a certain Loyal Goulding from Cork Golf Club. He has his own story to tell about how he got into "heaven" once, and has been going back every year since. The same Mr. Goulding, if he happens to meet anybody from Ireland at Augusta, has been known to dismiss them with a wave of his hand, which can be interpreted as follows: "Go away. I can talk to you at home. Time is too valuable for me to waste it talking to you here!"

The on-course "cabins" where President Eisenhower and Bob Jones used to stay are totally unpretentious. The Par-3 course beyond the surprisingly small practice ground is breathtakingly beautiful. The holes wind their way around a lovely lake in a tree-lined valley. You can get really close to the players and there is a lot of banter and fun between them and the spectators that would never be contemplated during the tournament proper. Augusta's beauty is legendary and familiar to all keen golf watchers, but TV does not do it full justice. The flowers and shrubs are a riot of gorgeous colours, helped no doubt by the fact that the property was actually a nursery before it was turned into a golf course. The spectators are colourful too, and noticeably more boisterous than a British or Irish crowd. We saw numerous "enthusiastic" parties taking place in the mammoth car parks near the course.

If something exciting happens way down in the valley at the twelfth and thirteenth it is quite extraordinary the way the reaction of the crowd wafts its way up to the clubhouse 1,000 feet above. The crowd, which gathers around the glorious sixteenth, seems to create a sound and atmosphere all its own. There is a birdie cheer, a par-saving cheer, a chip-in roar and the dreaded murmur. Murmurs are bad news. Augusta veterans sitting by the clubhouse can interpret the cheers and murmurs coming from the valley below with unerring accuracy. They could tell you that is a Nicklaus cheer or a Palmer murmur as the case may be. There is a standard joke that if there is a particularly loud cheer down below, a wag would say, "Arnie must have hitched his pants again."

I get butterflies in my stomach all over again, just thinking about it.

On the Monday morning after the tournament, it was time to go home. We had to fly from Augusta to Atlanta on the first leg of the journey. While waiting for our flight, we realized the plane was going to be full of golf personalities of world renown. We agreed amongst ourselves that our famous fellow passengers were now private citizens and entitled not to be bothered. When we took our seats on the plane, Marie found herself sitting across the aisle, within touching distance of Seve Ballesteros. He had his Spanish manager sitting with him and they chatted noisily and non-stop in their rapid-fire native tongue. During the short journey, Marie was reading the morning issue of the Augusta *Chronicle*. On the cover there was a half-page colour picture of Seve helping Tom Watson to put on the winner's green jacket. Suddenly, out of the blue, Seve tapped Marie on the shoulder. She nearly passed out with fright. He indicated that he would like to borrow her newspaper. It was duly handed over. I whispered to Marie, "Now is your chance to get his autograph. Ask him to sign the picture when he gives back the newspaper."

Seve took a cursory look at the newspaper. He was only interested in the photograph, or perhaps could not read English, so he handed it back. At that point Marie asked him to sign. You would have thought the paper was electrified. Seve behaved like a startled rabbit. He as good as threw the newspaper at her and refused point blank. Fr. Enright, who was in the window seat, with me in the middle, went ballistic and noisily threatened all sorts of misfortune upon the Spaniard. Marie was stunned into silence and said nothing, and it was lucky that she and I blocked the way because Fr. Gerry would have lacerated Seve, if he could have gone eyeball to eyeball with him. Considering Seve's own bellicose streak, there could easily have been a major in-flight incident and the newspaper headlines the next day would have been quite extraordinary:

Champion golfer and Parish Priest punch up in midair!

When we were getting off the plane in Atlanta, and things had cooled down, "the Manager" apologised rather tamely, saying that it was all a misunderstanding due to language difficulties, but still no autograph was offered.

Fr. Gerry's bad humour was soon banished by Ben Crenshaw whom we met in the Atlanta airport while waiting for our respective onward connections. When the Reverend saw Ben, he forgot our privacy pact and rushed straight up to him and blurted, "Can I please shake hands with the greatest putter in the world?"

Ben was charming. He referred to the fifteenth hole at Portmarnock as being the shortest par five in the world. He said this because it is only 180 yards long and he had made two fives on it during the course of the Irish Open in 1976, but still managed to win the tournament. I had a lot of fun telling him that I had comprehensively outscored him at the same hole during the same tournament. The fact that I had missed the halfway cut was not mentioned of course. (How sad and sickened I was to see another side of "Gentle

Ben," winding up his fellow countrymen, players and spectators alike, into a frenzy at "a little exhibition" match between the U.S. and Europe at Brookline in September of 1999. It was so different from the "nice man" we met at the airport, and totally out of keeping with his public persona.)

Finally, the town of Augusta itself appeared far from friendly and heavenly when we had our first sight of it on arrival at midnight on the previous Sunday. We had extreme difficulty finding a taxi and when we did, we were ill at ease in the company of a most fierce and suspect-looking fellow. We could not understand one word he said in his bluegrass accent, nor did he appear to understand our Irish brogues either. We drove around for what seemed like ages through some pretty scary and inhospitable looking neighborhoods before finally being deposited safely on the O'Neill's doorstep. It is hard to believe that one of the worlds most beautiful and heavenly golf courses is located in such grim and hellish surroundings. Augusta National Golf Club is on Bobby Jones Highway, a street that is honky-tonk America at its fluorescent worst. When you enter Magnolia Lane, however, you are in an entirely different world.

⊛

CHAPTER 2

Back to the Beginning
Catching the golf bug

"It is a crying shame!"

"What's a shame?" says I, puzzled.

"You," says Murphy.

"What did I do?" says I.

"It is a shame you gave up rugby so young. You could have played for Ireland if you had stayed with it. To hell with this crazy golf game!"

This conversation took place in the middle of a golf match that I was playing for Munster against Wales at Douglas Golf Club, Cork, in 1981. Noel "Noisy" Murphy, the infamous, former Irish rugby captain and coach, was a spectator following the match in which I was involved. As we walked up the hill at the ninth hole, Noisy came up beside me and launched into his opening gambit. That allowed me to tell Murphy that he was partly responsible for my decision to quit. Now, *he* was puzzled. You see, the very first competitive rugby game I played after leaving school in 1964 was for Old Crescent against Murphy's all-conquering Cork Constitution side in the Munster Senior League. Selected to play at outside-half, I was directly in the firing line of the best back row in Ireland at the time (Liam Coughlan, Gerry Murray, and Noel Murphy)—a daunting

Early competition, winning a footrace in 1960.

prospect for a seasoned international, let alone a callow youth just out of rompers like myself. Against other schoolboys, I was well able to take care of myself. But matching wits and physique with these mature brutes was a different matter. Early in the game we won a lineout in mid-field and the ball came to me rather more slowly than it should have— a "hospital pass" if ever there was one! Murphy, who must have been fifty pounds heavier and five inches taller than I was, caught me by the scruff of the neck and manhandled me to such an extent that I was thrown head over heels like a tumbleweed back down the field toward my own goal line. Before I could get back on my feet and gather my equilibrium, Murphy arrived on the scene. Towering over me, he "politely" asked, "Are you okay, young fellow?"

"I am," says I.

"Well," says he, "stay away from the blankety ball or I will break your blankety-blank neck!"

I took him at his word, and for the rest of the game made absolutely sure to follow his crystal clear instructions. Any time the ball came to hand I immediately kicked it to the farthest corner of the pitch. When I told Murphy about this later, he roared with laughter.

Of course, that was not the real reason I gave up a promising rugby career, but it coloured my thinking, shall we say. What really happened was that I missed all of the 1965–66 rugby season because I was at Eckerd College in Florida. While there, I played on the golf team and became totally immersed and besotted by the game. Winter golf in Florida was intoxicating. The weather and course conditions were so superior compared to home that I just could not get enough of it. By the time I returned to Ireland my handicap had dropped to one and I was considering an offer from Roland Stafford to turn professional and "see how good I might become." Another option was to accept a golf scholarship from the University of Houston and play for their famous coach, Dave Williams. But the Vietnam War was at its height and I would have made myself liable for the draft if I changed my visa status. Like Cassius Clay before me, I had "nuthin' against them Vietcongs." So I declined the opportunity. I have had to live with tinges of regret about that decision ever since, but I made my mind up at the time and that was that. The bridge was burned. As for rugby, I had become so interested in golf that I just did not want to spend my time playing with oval balls anymore. It was not the game itself that influenced me as much as being "marooned" by the off-field antics of my rugby colleagues. I took my golf seriously, and late nights of drinking beer and other nefarious activities after matches in Dublin, Cork, or Belfast were of no use to my developing golf career.

My last game of rugby took place in Dublin against St. Mary's College in November 1967. It was a lousy, windswept day and we were thrashed. Playing at full back, the last line of defence, I found myself trying to prevent a tidal wave of blue shirts going past me. But the unkindest cut of all was that a number of my teammates—wimps on the field of play—became devils off it and went "missing" on a rampage around the pubs of Dublin's Fair City after the game. Our team bus was supposed to leave at 9:00 P.M. and arrive back in Limerick around midnight. Understandably, the team captain, Jim Foley, would not allow the bus to leave without his missing "warriors." Eventually we arrived back in Limerick at 6:00 A.M., and I had an important golf match at 9:30 A.M. That was the last straw. I told Foley I was "history." He thought I was joking, but he and his successors spent the next four or five years trying to persuade me to change my mind. I stuck firmly to my decision, eventually severing all links with rugby. I have not been to a game for years, and I rarely watch it on television. When I do, I am astounded at what a crude and violent game it appears to me now, and wonder what Jesuit propaganda attracted me to it in the first place.

This is a book about golf. But in view of my former rugby days, I think my readers might indulge me and allow one more story. It is supposed to have taken place at the conclusion of a typically rough local derby match in my hometown, where the rugby is of a very coarse variety indeed. Two famous, revered front-row forwards, John "Pako" Fitzgerald and Peter "The Claw" Clohessy, were gingerly leaving the "Killing Fields," as their home ground is affectionately, but not inaccurately, known.

"Janey Pako, I have two fierce sore balls here!"

"Really, Claw, whose are they?"

I began golf in earnest in 1961, just short of my sixteenth birthday. Until then there was little time for it in my busy sporting life. I was aware of it all right because my Mum and Dad played. My three brothers and I foozled around in the yard and played a little Pitch and Putt (par-3 golf, Irish style) at nearby Ardnacrusha. But I was too involved in other sports, especially rugby and soccer, to be able to find time for golf as well. Rugby was my winter game and soccer my summer game. Any overlapping caused conflict at school because rugby was treated like a religion and soccer

Summerville Rovers, 1957. The author is in the front row at the far left.

was frowned upon. The Jesuits had a class bias against soccer, which was completely unjustified and rightly ridiculed by my father. Occasionally I was "picked upon" at school by Jesuits who should have known better because of my involvement in soccer. To further confuse matters I was teased for being "the college boy" on the soccer fields by colleagues and opponents, some of whom would not have been all that far removed from the deprived circumstances of Frank McCourt of *Angela's Ashes* fame. For example, I am sure I was one of the few soccer players who had the luxury of underpants back then. It was all a bit perplexing, but it did not influence me to stop. It all came to a head when I was selected to play for the Irish Schoolboys soccer team against England on the day after Crescent College had an important rugby game against Belvedere College in Dublin. I refused to play for the school so that I would be injury-free for the soccer match. One Jesuit in particular did not appreciate being told that I might only receive one chance to play for my country whereas I could play for my school any time. I suffered badly for that insolence for quite a while afterward.

It was not unusual for me to play both a rugby game and a soccer game on the same day, but I dared not tell the Jesuits. Competitive swimming, hockey, athletics, and tennis were also indulged in at various times. I achieved some success at all of them, in a local context at least. After I gave up rugby, hockey became a most useful and pleasurable way to keep fit during the dark winter months. I liked hockey because we mostly played at night "under lights," and it therefore did not interfere with my golfing activities. I played it enthusiastically until I twisted knee ligaments at age 41 and decided that enough was enough.

I am very proud of two Munster Schools Rugby Cup medals won with Crescent College in 1961 and 1963. Such victories give a schoolboy valuable self-confidence and show him early in life the value of focus and discipline and the importance of sticking to your guns through thick and thin. I can remember vividly how we plotted those triumphs. We were by no means the most skilful bunch of guys but we were well organised: Everyone knew his task and never deviated from it. We concentrated on "blanket defence" and we did not concede a single touchdown for over four months in 1963 and possibly twenty games in all. I was also selected to play for a very successful Munster Schools rugby team, the highlights of which were an unbeaten tour of Wales in 1964 and a mauling of Leinster Schools in Dublin. During this game I managed to kick an unforgettable wind-assisted 63-yard field goal. There was no Irish Schools rugby team at the time, so I do not know how that lost opportunity might have affected later developments. In late 1962 our regular rugby coach at the Crescent, Father Guinane S.J., became ill. The top Jesuit rugby coach in Ireland, Father Tom "The Bull" O'Callaghan S.J., was seconded from Belvedere College in order to take charge of us and hopefully guide us to victory. It amused me greatly to hear many years later that when O'Callaghan arrived incognito to watch his new team without being introduced to anybody, he asked of his Jesuit

Crescent College, 1961 Munster Schools Rugby Cup champions. Young Ivan is kneeling third from right.

companion, "Who is the out-half? He has got a distinct Protestant air about him!"

It was me, of course, and the irony was that I have always been proud of the Protestant and Catholic blood that flows through my veins. I was even more pleased some years later to further verify "the Bull's" observation when I followed my Dad's footsteps and took to the hockey field in the cardinal and white stripes of LPYMA (Limerick Protestant Young Men's Association), the first Catholic ever to do so. That was an offence for which I am unlikely to lose my soul, in spite of what the Jesuits' might have said back in 1962.

After the Irish Schoolboys soccer team played England at Highfield Road in Coventry in April of 1961, I was offered a month's trial by Aston Villa, the famous English club. Dad, unfortunately, put his foot down and would not allow me to go over to Birmingham. That disappointment caused a few twinges of regret, too. But looking back, it was the correct decision and it is understandable why he took the attitude he did. I was a reasonably good student and there was not a lot of money to be earned as a professional

With younger brother Dermot, 1961.

soccer player in 1961. There was a maximum wage limit of
£20 per week. That was not bad at the time, but it hardly
compares with what footballers earn nowadays and you
could not secure your future on it. Much and all as I loved
soccer, the role of an apprentice cleaning the boots of the
first team players and sweeping out the dressing rooms and
stands after matches—the type of lifestyle described by
Eamon Dunphy in his classic bestseller *Only A Game?* (published first in 1976 by Viking Books in London, and now
available several reprints later from Penguin)—would
hardly have appealed to my puritanical and middle class
upbringing. For example, I learned later that soccer players
drink even more than ruggers! With hindsight, the pagan,
immoral lifestyle of a professional footballer in England
would not have suited me one little bit. My Dad wanted me
to complete my School Leaving Certificate and join him in
his business of running a local weekly newspaper and printing works. A true Corinthian, he said I should concentrate

on sport as an amateur and play for fun and a sense of achievement. He did not believe in professional sport. He encouraged his four sons' sporting activities enthusiastically, but always in an amateur context. All of the cash and career opportunities, which came into sport later, were hardly imagined as a possibility by him in 1961. He would be staggered by what top professional sportsmen earn these days. No doubt he would have asked, "What value does that put on a surgeon?" When I wondered out loud about the feasibility and wisdom of going to Loughborough College in England to study physical education, my musings were greeted with a rare wallop with a rolled up newspaper and I was told with some vehemence to "have a bit of sense!"

One of my Dad's sporting heroes was triple international star Dr. Kevin O'Flanagan, who played soccer for Arsenal in the English Football League. Kevin managed to remain an amateur while still pursuing a medical career in London. He also found time to play on the wing for the Ireland rugby team and ran in the 1948 London Olympics. That was pretty impressive, and it was always being held up to me as something I should try to emulate. My Dad was thrilled when I actually played golf with Kevin in the East of Ireland Amateur Golf Championship at Baltray in 1970. It was long after Kevin had retired from athletics, soccer, and rugby. He told me he regretted not having the time to take up golf earlier than he did, because "it was possibly the best game of all." Today, at 81, Kevin remains a stylish if quick-swinging golfer. I observed him playing as enthusiastically as ever at Portmarnock with a trio of equally sprightly old gents in May of 2000. For a man who had played regularly at Highbury and Lansdowne Road in front of fifty odd thousand people, Kevin is surprisingly nervous and highly strung in the wide-open spaces of a golf course.

All the sports that I played were of assistance to my golf, and I made very rapid progress, reaching 10 handicap by the end of my first summer at it. One year later I was down to 5 and becoming hooked. From the beginning I had good

My dad, the athlete, 1939.

hand and eye coordination, understood how to propel the
ball, had a feel for distance, and knew how to compete. I
was always keen to play with better players than myself so
that I could observe them at close quarters and learn. I also
enjoyed the fact that you could play golf on your own without an opponent or companion. The strategies of golf fascinated me right from the very beginning. Figuring out the
best way to play a new course or hole exercised me. I also
loved nothing better than to hit balls quietly on my own on
the practice ground, experimenting and imagining all sorts
of situations. I would still do so more often if I did not have
to pick up the balls!

There were several other factors that stoked up my passion for golf. The greatest, without doubt, was the influence of my golf-playing parents and brothers. Then there
was the late Father Gerry Enright, a larger than life charac-

Father Enright in 1946.

ter who had a vast knowledge of most sports, but particularly golf. He was a fitness fanatic who adored being out in
the fresh air, walking, golfing, or swimming. He was an
enthusiastic advocate of "temperance," and firmly believed
that a healthy body was "the product of what we put into
it." He used to say, "A healthy body is the citadel of a healthy
mind." I believed him, and still do. As soon as he had completed his daily duties he was at one of his energetic pas-
times. Father Enright's passion for golf was well known in
Rathkeale, where he was curate for many years. If he was
not at Ballyclough or Ballybunion playing golf he was in a
field close to the town lashing balls into the far distance,
scaring the cows! He was a big hitter and very proud of it.
Whenever he saw somebody hit an exceptional shot, he
would mark the spot and come back later to see if he could
match it. After a visit to the Vatican he described St. Peter's

Square as "a good belt of a four iron" when trying to illus-trate the dimensions of it to a bemused clerical friend.

We bumped into each other on the course at Ballyclough one fine summer afternoon in 1961 when he was a rather awesome (to me) 2 handicapper. We played nonstop until darkness fell. It was the beginning of an intense friendship in spite of the wide disparity in our ages. We regularly played 54 holes in a day, and anything less than 36 holes was considered "useless." Forty-five holes became our regular diet. It would be impossible to play that much now because of traffic on the course. If we were doing one of our 45-hole stints, we would play 27 "practice holes" and then stop for refreshments before getting down to the "serious business" of doing a score. The food we ate always consisted of brown soda bread, scones, and buttermilk, and an apple, tomato, or banana for dessert. We ate while sitting on the grass at the back of the old wooden clubhouse, with the latest golf magazine from America being digested with the same gusto as the food. Before teeing off, we always negotiated a target score. Sometimes if things did not go well over the first few holes, and the coast was clear, we would rush back to the first tee and begin again! We used to play for a half a crown (12.5 pence) or a golf ball. First it was a "Silver King" and later a "Penfold." Back in the early 1960s, the latter was the ultimate in golf ball style. It featured markings denot-ing playing cards—for example, the ace of spades rather than a number. Neither one of us was fond of losing; we both strained mightily to win. Father Gerry's often-declared definition of happiness was "to be three up on Ivan Morris and my office said!" That was some compliment I can assure you, because Roman Catholic priests have a prayer book that they jokingly refer to as their "office." At some quiet moment of convenience during every day they medi-tate by reading a predetermined prayer or reflection—sim-ilar to reading the "psalm of the day," I suppose. It usually takes about fifteen minutes to fulfill this priestly obligation.

Father Gerry and I never bothered with conventional

handicaps; we made up our own games, or tried to achieve a nominated gross score. We rewarded and penalized each other for being above or below target. We each had a small tin box of tees in our golf bags (hickies, we called them) and they were in constant use as chits, for "fairways and greens hit," "sandies," and "P's" and "S's" (being past the flag or short of it). We think we might have invented a game later to become known as "Recall." That was a fantastic training exercise, especially for me. It comprised of granting each other a certain number of licences to recall a bad shot played, or, even more interestingly, forcing the opposition to replay an especially good one. That caused a lot of extra pressure, I can assure you. My clerical friend was very hard on me and his stock of tees grew as mine dwindled. But I knew such training was good for me and I would learn more from losing than winning. Father Gerry kept a detailed diary of every game we played. But I was never allowed to see what was written down about our titanic struggles. I wonder what unflattering name he called me the day I holed out a nine-iron from about 120 yards at the eighteenth at Ballyclough with himself "stone dead" beside the hole and one up. Our games were that competitive.

The idea of a target score (which I picked up from Father Enright) was of great help to me years later when I was coaching Limerick Golf Club teams for Irish Cup and Shield matches. In my opinion, trial matches between teammates are a waste of time. You learn nothing from them. Instead, the "invisible man" was conceived for the squad to compete against. "He" was a holy terror, with the uncanny ability to score half a shot at a vital hole, doubling the pressure. One putt could mean the difference between winning and losing, as halved holes were out of the equation. There was no comfort zone. I found it very revealing of a player's character to see how he reacted to this situation. Players buckle at every level of the game. Pressure is a mental thing. Some learn to cope better than others. The invisible man was highly efficient at identifying who could and who could not be

In action during the Munster Boys Championship in 1963.

trusted. Even highly paid professionals cannot cope with being a winner or a loser every time they play. They will protest that they are in the glory and entertainment business, but most of them play like accountants with profit in mind and avoid risks. They aim to finish in the top ten for a nice paycheck. Believe it or not, winning is a bonus that is not worth the hassle for many touring professionals.

My passion for golf, aided and abetted by Father Enright, got me into more hot water with the Jesuits. On certain days at school, I had the job of ringing the bell between classes. I devised a scheme where I would "perform" as usual at 2:50 P.M. on Friday afternoons. Instead of going back to my boring Irish class, I would sneak out the back gate to where Father Gerry was waiting in his beige Volkswagen. We would speed off to Ballyclough or Ballybunion and our round would be well under way before my classmates were "released." Inevitably, we were caught in the act. Poor Father Gerry was highly embarrassed and he begged me to get a good result in my end of term exam, which fortunately I did, so all was forgiven.

Father Gerry was as much a terror behind the steering wheel as he was on the golf course. He drove his car with the same aggressive abandon as he wielded his Willie Daly persimmon driver. He would have driven the Volks straight through a field if he thought it would have helped him to get to his destination (usually the first tee) a moment sooner. One evening we were coming home from Ballybunion in the dark, and he turned off the car headlights as we approached the notorious Liselton Cross and began combing his hair. When I shrieked "What are you doing?" He told me not to worry, that he had been "going through Liselton for thirty years and never met anything!" He had turned off the lights "just to make sure nothing was coming." When I said there could have been a bicycle, or an animal on the road, he looked flummoxed. One of his parishioners, who travelled with him regularly, gently admonished him for his speedy driving by saying, "Do you know, Father, that there is not a dog or a cat left standing on the roads between Rathkeale, Ballybunion. and Limerick?" The significance went right over his head.

Father Enright also had a major influence on my decision to "retire" from rugby at the age of twenty-one. Over and over he kept telling me with some passion that golf could be played to a highly competitive standard up to an unspecified ripe old age, whereas a rugby career could barely last beyond 30 — if you were lucky. He told me the country was full of old rugby players like himself broken down by injuries — not to mention the pains and aches from all the knocks given and taken. As well as that, the heavy training associated with rugby makes your upper body muscle-bound and inflexible. Excessive upper body strength, which cultivates an expanded chest, is a handicap to a golfer.

My reverend friend's advice was very wise, but to quit was

not easy in a rugby-mad environment like Limerick. After I had stopped playing, several clubs tried to entice me back by telling me they would make it "worth my while" if I turned out for them. As this was long before the era of professionalism in rugby, I have no idea what they had in mind, but I was not remotely tempted. The soccer fell by the wayside also, as golf took up all of my time and gradually became my entire raison d'être. To a certain extent, it still is.

Father Enright had a subscription to the weekly American magazine *Golf World*—quite a rare matter in Ireland in the 1960s. When he had finished with the latest issue, which arrived three or four weeks after publication, he would pass it on to me. We would have no idea whatsoever who would have won the latest tournament in the U.S. until the magazine arrived. It was as good as today's news to us. We eagerly looked forward to each issue, and whenever the magazine arrived late, or out of sequence, there was consternation, and woe betide the unfortunate postman! Little did Dick Taylor, Ron Coffman, and their team of writers realize they had two such dedicated fans in County Limerick. Father Gerry also had a fine library of golf books, which he systematically lent to me. They were all read with relish. I am extremely grateful that before he died he left instructions that his golf books should be given to me.

Another inspiration was the television series *Shell's Wonderful World of Golf.* The show was initially made for viewing in America and distributed to golf clubs around the world as a promotion for the Shell Oil Company. The series was so popular that when infant Irish Television began broadcasting it, every keen golfing family in the country, like ours, rushed out to buy a television set. Prior to the home TV age, the Shell Representative in Limerick was Noel Harris, a younger brother of the famous actor, Richard Harris. Noel was a keen and stylish golfer at Ballyclough. He used his influence to get a copy of the latest Shell golf match, and it would be shown to a packed and awestruck clubhouse audience during the winter evenings. It was the highlight of my week. I used to go to the first tee on Saturday mornings to try to emulate the vivid mental pictures I had of Byron Nelson's dip, Don January's languid rhythm, or Peter Thomson's economical, simple style, to name but three of the many stars of *Shell's Wonderful World of Golf.*

Peter Thomson was a particular favourite of mine. He used to aim his left shoulder at the target while relaxing the right side of his body. He played position golf and was always in full control of the ball. I loved watching him play. I followed him loyally at Woodbrook during the Carroll's Tournament in the 1960s. My first set of matched irons was a Peter Thomson set by Dunlop that I bought a few clubs at a time over a period of several months from Denis Cassidy, the popular and wise professional at Castletroy Golf Club. Only the super rich could afford to buy a full set at one time. Denis built up a huge business by offering this service. Golfers came to him from far and wide for the best deals in Ireland. He cornered the market by allowing his customers the most generous credit terms. Those Thomson irons cost two pounds, twelve shillings, and six pence per club (£2.62p.). The last club I bought to complete the set of 2 iron through sand wedge was the pitching wedge. Can you imagine playing without a pitching wedge? But I do give myself a little credit for buying the sand club early in the process. It was Denis Cassidy who gave me my first formal professional lesson. I can still remember his clear and forceful instructions: "Hang on hard with your left hand and bate the buckin' ball!" he thundered. That simple piece of advice is just as effective today as it undoubtedly was all those years ago.

There was a lively clubhouse discussion after each Shell show, and I used to love to listen to the club's best players at the time, Patrick J. Walsh, Nick McMahon, and Garry Geary, analysing the techniques of the performers. One evening we were all stunned by the sight of Pine Valley. There were gasps of astonishment as the various hazards of the hole about to be played were described. First, a very basic outline of the hole was shown on screen, then one by one the trees, traps, and water hazards were painted in. By the time all the hazards had been included we were nearly on our knees begging for mercy. Little did I realise that I would have the opportunity to play this fabulous course thirty-five years later and it was not half as frightening as I expected it to be.

Sky Sports TV has been showing these old *Shell's Wonderful World of Golf* film classics recently, and it is also possible to purchase VCR versions for home viewing. It is perfectly obvious how much the game has changed and how much the courses and players have improved since the 1960s and 70s.

❀

CHAPTER 3

An Insider's Guided Tour of Irish Golf

I suppose it is not for me to say, but golf in Ireland is special. Nor do you have to take my word for it. This is what Philadelphia author James W. Finegan has to say about it:

From the opening drive at Lahinch, just thirty miles from your arrival point at Shannon Airport, to the spectacular dune-framed holes at Ballybunion, Ireland boasts an extraordinary collection of seaside links. Royal County Down, Royal Portrush, Portmarnock, Portstewart, Waterville, The Island, The European Club and Baltray—any of these would be reason to cross an ocean.

The concentration of all of these great links, and more, in an area no bigger than the state of Maine, means you can play a marvellous variety of courses in a short space of time—and without having to travel thousands of miles. The roads in Ireland used to be fairly scary, but not anymore, unless you go well off the beaten track. Actually, that is where I am going to take you, part of the time, on my own "Insider's Tour of Irish Golf." There will be a heavy emphasis on seaside links golf, but not exclusively so. I regularly bring my American friends to the venues mentioned and they always go home with smiles of satisfaction on their faces. Because of occasional conflict with local competitions and pressure on tee times, there has to be the odd compromise or two. We will make allowances for that by putting more on your plate than you can possibly digest. One American I know gives his fellow countrymen the sound advice that the best way to enjoy Ireland is to "go with the flow" and "do as the Romans do." He was getting his metaphors mixed up, but it is nevertheless appropriate and sound advice.

One of the most interesting cultural differences between Ireland and the U.S. is the proliferation of local talk radio stations all over the country. They are of widely differing standards. Some are very professional, others quite amateurish. Kerry Radio has produced its fair share of Mrs. Malaprop gems. One of their sports announcers may be an expert on hurling and Gaelic football, but his knowledge of Grand Prix motor racing and golf is not up to par. While driving home from Ballybunion a couple of years ago, I heard that Michael "Shoemaker" had won a race somewhere and that Davis Love had won the MCI Heritage Classic with the great score of "one hunderd and eleven," while Frank "Nobbobillio" was runner-up in the same event. How that announcer would have coped if Mark Calcavecchia were involved is anybody's guess. When driving around the country, take my advice and spin the dial and listen to the local radio stations. You are certain to be entertained and likely to be educated as well. Very often there are highly cerebral, thought-provoking programs on almost any subject under the sun. My friend Bill Schackel and I were intrigued while driving home from Ballybunion one evening by a well researched program called "Outlaws of the Wild West with Irish Connections," presented by Myles Dungan of RTE. Right there and then I was able to take a slight detour to show Bill the village of Asdee, located halfway between Ballybunion and Tarbert. Jesse James's ancestors emigrated to the American west from this rather sleepy, inoffensive County Kerry village.

I am going to give you two possible itineraries: one for those who arrive in Shannon and wish to stay in the west and south, and another for those who arrive in Dublin and are prepared to travel a wider area. You can, of course, mix and match or cherry pick to your heart's desire, depending on the amount of time at your disposal and whether you are prepared to do the extra driving involved.

Based on personal experience, I think visiting golfers should find themselves a reasonably central headquarters and confine their activities to an area not exceeding an 80-mile radius. It is more enjoyable to get to know an area well—especially the people—rather than dashing helter-skelter all over the place.

Because tee times at the better known venues are in such demand and short supply, I would strongly suggest that you get one of the professional golf services companies—such as Golf Tours or SWING—to arrange them for you *long before* your departure date. These organizations can book a limited number of tee times in advance at *no extra cost.* They will also arrange your accommodation, if you wish. (I have no connection whatsoever with these companies, apart from being a satisfied customer.) They have helped my friends and me innumerable times.

Shannon Arrivals

From the airport, drive for 45 minutes straight to Lahinch and have a truly wonderful introduction to what Irish golf is all about. It is important to play through the jet lag, and not retire until your normal bedtime at home. The combination of fatigue and stinking fresh air will have you sleeping like a top, and you will find your "Irish legs" all the sooner. In order to be able to do this, it is probably imperative to grab forty winks during the flight over. The only way to achieve that successfully may be to take a sleeping pill. If you can manage to sleep on the airplane it will make a big difference to your well-being and your ability to play on arrival.

The Village of Lahinch is known as "the St. Andrews of Ireland," and it is almost entirely golf-oriented. The royal and ancient game permeates the atmosphere to an extent that is only matched at "headquarters" in Scotland. You are even likely to receive an overdose of detailed and highly intelligent golf advice from your host at breakfast, whether you ask for it or not!

There are so many B&B accommodations of excellent standards available all over Ireland that there is no need to look for four-star hotel accommodation—that is, unless you have money to burn. Many of the B&Bs are every bit as good as a fine hotel, at a fraction of the cost.

On your second morning you could drive just north of Galway City to a new course called Bearna. It should take about an hour and a half to get there along the scenic coastal route, but allow more time than that, so that you can stop and view the Cliffs of Moher, the exotic orchids of the Burren country, the six-thousand-year-old Ailwee Caves in North Clare, or one of the pretty villages along the way, such as Ballyvaughan or Kinvara. Not too far away there is a Heritage Center at Corofin that is well worth visiting if you have the time and interest in tracing relatives who may have emigrated to America in famine times. Or if Greg Norman's Doonbeg is open for play—which it might be by the time you are reading this—by all means go there instead. Some of the best pub grub in Ireland is available at Morrisseys, close to the Doonbeg course. Also close to Doonbeg is the little town of Miltown-Malbay. There you'll find some of the best pubs in the country for traditional Irish music and sing-alongs.

Bearna is a delight. It is not a seaside links but bog-land golf. Never heard of such a thing? Well, neither did I until recently, but it was great. It was like playing in the Everglades without the heat, snakes, and alligators. The course is in the middle of nowhere. Such peace and tranquillity is rare nowadays. If you come from a big metropolis you will love it. You can almost hear the bees farting, as a famous Lahinch golfer, Mick O'Loughlin, used to say. Bearna calls for good straight golf, without being crushingly difficult. You will appreciate that, as jet lag is always worse on the second day.

For the purposes of holiday golf in Ireland, I would recommend that visiting golfers use the ingenious "Bolene Method of Scoring." My friend Bruce Bolene, from Santa Fe, New Mexico, is a regular visitor to these shores. He carries a plus-one handicap and is therefore well qualified to understand the difficulties of playing to one's handicap in strange surroundings. Some time ago he devised his own staggeringly simple scoring system for "on the road." If you ask him what score he shot, he will come up with an answer like "9-4-5." That means nine good holes, four mediocre ones, and five poor ones. That is all the detail you will get! If Bruce can shoot twelve or more "good ones," he is ecstatic and liable to buy dinner. At home I am sure he is a little harder to please. This system makes a lot more sense than counting every backbreaking stroke—especially when I think of the day I was at Ballybunion with Michael Galvin. We nearly choked on our sandwiches when we overheard the following comments from a visiting "expert": "Hey, Cecil, I thought this Ballybunion was supposed to be a hard course. I have just added up my score and I shot 132 today. Yesterday at Killarney I shot 145. Killarney is a lot tougher!"

After Bearna, you have the choice of continuing north to play Connemara, Carn, Enniscrone, and Rosses Point. All are magnificent seaside tracks. Connemara is near the town of Clifden, which is famous for its Horse Fairs (sales). If there is one in progress during your visit, get involved, mingle, observe, and soak up the culture. About an hour north of Connemara is Carn, the masterpiece of Irish golf architect Eddie Hackett. It features some of the highest dunes in Irish golf. Slightly further north are Enniscrone and Rosses Point—both superb, tough links that have hosted the Irish National and West of Ireland Amateur Championships.

You can also begin my personal preferred route by coming back to Galway City to stay overnight. Galway is overflowing with "culture," of both an Irish and an international

This row of colorful and photogenic thatched cottages is located right beside the entrance gate to the Adare Manor and Golf Course in the pretty County Limerick village of Adare. (Michael Diggin Photography)

flavour. Next morning, head southwards to County Limerick. Be aware that there is an extremely confusing situation at Adare. On your way into the village you will see a sign that reads: "Adare Manor Golf Club." This is not your destination. Horseman, pass by! You want "The Adare Golf Club" on the Manor grounds, the gate of which is opposite the Dunraven Arms Hotel on the eastern entrance to one of Ireland's prettiest villages. I know it does not make sense, but that's the way it is.

If you decide to stay at the Dunraven Arms Hotel, you will find that the ambience and service both play off scratch at an establishment that has married the old and new magnificently. Or you could just as comfortably rest your bones at the recently opened Holiday Village in the Manor grounds, beside the golf course. There are also numerous excellent B&Bs in the village. The Adare Golf Club has a fine practice facility with a fully qualified PGA

The Dunraven Arms Hotel at Adare has a friendly atmosphere, service out of the top drawer and a dinner menu second to none. Travelling golfers and members of the fox hunting set are particularly well cared for.

Professional, Brian Shaw, in attendance. He is Irish-born but American-trained, and that puts the best of both worlds at your disposal. Having him teach you the quail high-wind cheater and the bump-and-run shot might be a good move with Ballybunion on the horizon. By all means make Adare your HQ for a couple of nights and commute to County Kerry. There is nothing worse than changing beds every night.

While at Adare you simply must play the last great course designed by the late Robert Trent Jones Sr., Adare Golf Club. It may be an American-style course, but it is a wonderful test in magnificent surroundings. The toughest opening par four imaginable, and what Mr. Jones himself described as "the best finishing par five hole in golf," are memorable features. The sight of the splendid gothic Manor House, which overlooks the finishing holes, is worth the green fee alone. The Manor is the baby of Adare's many historic buildings, having been built as recently as 1832. Within a mile of your hotel is a feast of mediaeval architecture. The ruins of the thirteenth-century Desmond Castle (1227) still stand on the river bank at the east entrance to the village, and are being carefully restored at present. Straight opposite on the other side of the road is the Black Abbey, originally an Augustinian Monastery built in 1315. It is now the parish home of the local Protestant community, and has been lovingly restored and cared for by them. On Main Street, beside the Dunraven Arms, is the still working Catholic Parish Church built in 1203 as a Trinitarian Monastery. In addition, the fifteenth-century Franciscan Friary is a hazard right in the middle of the privately owned and confusingly named Adare Manor Golf Course. The two Adare golf courses are side by side, but they are chalk and cheese. It is hard to believe that these buildings have been standing since before Columbus discovered the New World. There is an excellent view of the Franciscan Friary from the fourteenth green on the Trent Jones course. All of this history is well worth a look. Its survival is mainly due to the benefactions of successive Earls of Dunraven, who lived in the Manor until quite recently. Over the years, the Earls established a reputation for being generous and supportive of their peasant neighbours and staff. Time marches on, however, and even old wealth runs out eventually.

With Adare as your base, visit Ballybunion and Killarney next. You will need all your faculties for Ballybunion, so get plenty of rest the night before. If you are up for it, you might like to play both courses at Ballybunion in one day. But take a caddie: You will need all the help you can get on your way around. After golf, go to the town of Listowel and eat at Woulfe's Horseshoe Bar to enjoy the atmosphere of a lively Irish pub, which serves a wide choice of good food. Just up the street from Woulfe's is the writer John B. Keane's Public House. If the great man himself is *in situ*, you could be in for a few surprising and entertaining moments. He is a treasure, and he loves to perform for his

The typically tumbling nature of the two Ballybunion golf courses is clearly visible in this back-to-front Michael Diggin photograph of the first hole on the Cashen Course.

customers, reciting poetry and singing ballads.

There are three courses at Killarney. All are excellent, but I like to play a composite of Killeen's first sixteen and Mahony's last six whenever it is feasible to do so. You will not get a better stretch than that! Then retrace the beloved, late Payne Stewart's footsteps by going to Foley's Restaurant on Killarney's Main Street for sustenance. Tell Denis and Carol I sent you. Try the scallops or red gurnet.

If you are a mountaineering enthusiast, by all means go to the Ring of Kerry course at Templenoe near Kenmare. The scenery is magnificent but the golf course is unreasonably difficult to walk and play. Whoever laid it out was either a masochist or wanted to increase revenue by forcing golfers to use the carts, which are available for a fee. If you want to experience a really outstanding scenic drive—which in parts is not too unlike being on the surface of the moon—drive back over the mountains from Kenmare to

Only one of the several magnificent lakeside views across Laugh Leane on Killarney's beautiful and formidable Killeen Course. (Michael Diggin Photography)

Killorglin, which is home to "Nick's," one of the best seafood restaurants in Ireland. Its exotic and elaborate dishes jump straight out of the nearby Atlantic onto your plate.

If you feel like moving your base camp to Tralee at any stage, the Brook Manor Lodge on the Fenit Road is where you should stay. It is a superb purpose-built golfers' B&B. However, I cannot bring myself to recommend the Arnold Palmer–designed Tralee course at Barrow, north of the town, in spite of the magnificent scenery that surrounds it and the bush telegraph news that the course has matured nicely. Too many bad experiences in its early days have not yet been forgotten or forgiven. Instead I prefer to head for the Dingle Peninsula. The road through Conor Pass and down into Dingle is fabulous. On the way, just fifteen miles beyond Tralee, there is an absolute gem of a nine-hole links named Castlegregory. Under no circumstances should you miss sampling its refreshingly simple but rough charms. You might be lulled into thinking it is easy, but if you stray from the fairway it will mug you, rob you of all your golf balls, and destroy your every vestige of self-confidence. At the very least you will work up an appetite to eat "down

An aerial view of Dr. Arthur Spring's elemental and beguiling 9-hole course at Castlegregory on the Dingle Peninsula. Playing here is like going back in time to another era, when golf was far removed from the affluent status it "enjoys" today. There is room for another 27 holes at Castlegregory but unfortunately not the population to sustain it. (Michael Diggin Photography)

Tomasin's Bar is only one mile from the 1st tee of the Castlegregory Golf Course. The food and drink served in these humble but atmospheric surroundings—turf fires included—are as good as any five-star hotel.

A windswept scene at Ceann Sibeal, Europe's westernmost golf course. The eye-catching Blasket Islands and Atlantic Ocean scenery nearby could easily cause you to take your eye off the ball. (Michael Diggin Photography)

home style" at Tomashin's atmospheric little pub nearby before you continue on your journey west to Dingle.

The name of the golf course at Dingle town is Ceann Sibeal (Sybil's Head). It is the westernmost golf course in Europe. Designed and built by Christy O'Connor Jr., it is loosely modelled on St. Andrews in Scotland. I have been there twice, but have yet to strike a ball. Too many other things to do. My brother Brien plays at Ceann Sibeal regularly and loves it. It is often very windy, so be prepared. At this juncture I should warn you that travelling to Ireland without a warm flat cap, woollen sweater, rain pants, and light waterproof jacket is asking for trouble. But do not be surprised or disappointed if you only need them to keep chill-proof from the wind. All those tales about rainy Ireland are greatly exaggerated.

In Dingle, stay at Doyle's Bar and B&B on John Street. The food is five-star gorgeous. Fresh locally caught lobster is the speciality of the house. The atmosphere in down-

Sean Cluskey, owner of Doyle's Seafood Bar and B&B in the center of Dingle Town, County Kerry, shows off some of his merchandise.

town Dingle is quite extraordinary. Be sure to leave yourself with enough time to have a good look around. It has several extremely interesting cultural and historic features to be seen and studied. There is a wonderful bookshop off the main boulevard that doubles as a café. Dave Davis and I spent a whole afternoon there, loading up with books and coffee while soaking up the atmosphere. We found Dingle much too interesting a place to waste time playing golf.

On your way to the golf course, a visit to Louis Mulcahy's pottery shop to bring home a peace offering for all the fun you are having without your companion in life is essential. Also on the way are the remains of primitive sixth-century monastic "beehive" settlements, which are quite beyond the comprehension of most twenty-first-century humans. Drive another few miles further on to the Blasket Island Interpretative Centre, where you will learn about an extinct island culture and community, and a little about the Irish language in the process. I came away with the impression that the birth of Irish feminism could have taken place on the Blasket Islands, through a feisty lady named Peig Sayers.

Dooks Golf Club at Glenbeigh is next on our list. This is one of the oldest courses in Ireland, and it has changed little over the years. Built by the golf-mad Scottish Black Watch Regiment, it is a genuine throwback to former times, presenting problems and challenges that are out of place in modern golf. Still, it is fun to confront them once in a blue moon. The first six holes are a bit quirky and are squashed too close together, but from No.7 onwards it is an excellent test. Dooks is the ancestral home of the once endangered Natterjack toad. These little fellows can be quite noisy at dusk, when they seem to fancy themselves as operatic stars, like Kermit of Muppets fame.

Next we move on down to Waterville to visit Payne Stewart's favourite singing haunt, the Butler Arms. This is an old style hotel that specializes in good food and hospitality. The Waterville Golf Course is seriously tough and not for wimps. After a calm opening few holes, it gradually turns up the volume, and the finish is as hard as nails. If this course were in Scotland, they would hold the Open on it regularly.

County Cork is our next destination. The Old Head course at Kinsale is a jaw dropper of mega proportions, rivalling Pebble Beach for spectacular clifftop views and drama. Precariously built on a piece of rock jutting out into the Atlantic, three hundred feet above the sea, it is definitely not for anyone suffering from vertigo! The last time I was there I spent a fascinating twenty minutes watching from on high as a herd of basking sharks fed on plankton within thirty yards of the shore. On a visit to Old Head in 1999, Tiger Woods, Payne Stewart, Lee Jantzen, and Mark O'Meara played through a thick sea fog, loving every minute of it. When the fog suddenly cleared, Tiger decided to take on an impossible shot at No. 17. He tried to carry across a sea inlet to the green that overhangs the cliff ledge. His boyish squeal of delight when he failed was a side of Tiger not seen before in Ireland.

Kinsale is known as the gourmet capital of Ireland.

There is a bewildering choice of top class restaurants, with seafood to the fore, as it is a busy working fishing village. Stay at the Blue Haven Hotel or at any of the many B&Bs overlooking the colourful boat-filled bay.

Fota Island, venue of the 2001 Irish Open, is a fine modern parkland course not too far away, while Cork Golf Club at Little Island is one of my favourite golfing places in the entire world. Located on the Lee Estuary, it could be called the Black Diamond of Ireland, because the course runs through an abandoned quarry, just like its Florida cousin (Black Diamond Ranch). Dr. Alister MacKenzie, the architect of Augusta National and Cypress Point, designed the present routing back in 1927, so it is not surprising that it should be rated so highly. The holes along the estuary are marvellously enjoyable and give that part of the course a links feeling. The scenery is superb, with some activity—be it animal or mineral—always taking place along by the shore.

Ready to keep going? Shannon is two hours from Cork; Dublin is three and a half-hours away!

Dublin Arrivals
If you are travelling to Dublin by road from Cork or across the Atlantic by air, make your first target stop Kilkenny. It is a lovely city with ancient walls and a Norman castle in the middle of downtown. The Jack Nicklaus–designed Mount Juliet is close by. The hotel there is the most wonderful place to stay, but the golf course is greatly overrated, like many Nicklaus courses, in my opinion. However, make sure to sample the 36-hole putting course. I enjoyed it more than the "big Momma," and thought it was well worth travelling all the way across Ireland to play it.

The European Club in County Wicklow is about one hour north of Kilkenny and thirty miles south of Dublin. It overlooks Brittas Bay on the Irish Sea. This is a big links that is only for serious golfers who do not whine. Some of the holes feature unusual and original thinking and compare with the best anywhere. Owner Pat Ruddy, who designed

The 8th green at the European Club, County Wicklow.

and built it, has a mean and nasty architectural style. In the clubhouse, he has a more pleasant and welcoming nature.

Portmarnock, just north of Dublin, was home to Harry Bradshaw for many years. It is the fairest test of seaside golf that I know. It bestows the correct value on every shot—good, bad, or indifferent. While the course is flat and doesn't have the drama, dunes, and scenery of Lahinch or Ballybunion, it is a lot tougher to play than either of them because of its greater length and more severe bunkering. Portmarnock has wonderful greens that are nearly always in excellent condition. It is a shame the Ryder Cup is not being played at Portmarnock in 2005 instead of at the rather "ordinary" parkland K-Club. Unfortunately, money talked louder than golfing considerations. Anyway, I could not see the sensible members of Portmarnock tolerating the hype involved.

You can stay quite comfortably and conveniently at the Portmarnock Links Hotel nearby, where there is a new course built by Bernhard Langer. A bit like the Adare situation in County Limerick, the course is confusingly called Pormarnock Links. This course is littered with grave-like fairway traps. I call them that because there is no way to get out of them! Portmarnock Links is fun to play if you can avoid those traps, but I much prefer to go to the Island Golf Club, which is not too far away as the crow flies. It predates "the original" Portmarnock and is on similar terrain. The Island is a highly enjoyable traditional links, featuring a number of blind holes. The thirteenth hole is one of the best par threes in all of Ireland.

Thirty-five miles further north is the County Louth Golf Club at Baltray. Be careful, because the road from Drogheda town to the course is twisty and dangerous, but it is well worth the effort. Baltray is a gem. There is limited accommodation available in the clubhouse. The East of Ireland Championship is played at Baltray on the first weekend in June each year, and it always provides an excellent test for Ireland's best golfers and a few brave challengers from overseas.

Royal County Down Golf Club at Newcastle, County Down, is not too far over the border in Northern Ireland. Without question, this is the best course in Ireland. It calls for powerful, straight hitting from the tee and precision

The 9th fairway at Royal County Down is truly one of the most amazing sights in golf. (Courtesy of Golfer's Companion magazine)

iron play. The back nine may not be quite as spectacular as the outward journey, but scoring low is not any easier. Nor is it the friendliest of clubs off the course, either. Visitors are not allowed in the clubhouse unless a member accompanies them. The course is too good to miss, however, and who cares about the clubhouse and the membership anyway? The town of Newcastle is quite attractive for a night's stay. I like the Burndale Lodge, but the silver turrets of the Slieve Donard Hotel are so convenient to the golf course that they are difficult to resist.

Next day, take the Antrim Coast road to the north. It is a fabulous, scenic drive, every bit as good as the Ring of Kerry, in my view. By all means visit the Bushmills Distillery and the Giant's Causeway on the way. The double whammy of Royal Portrush and Portstewart await you on arrival. Portrush is the only course in Ireland to have hosted the Open Championship (Max Faulkner was victorious in 1951). The par three holes are particularly memorable. Each of them plays to a different point on the compass, climaxing at No.14, the intimidating and aptly named Calamity Corner. The Valley course at Portrush is also well worth playing if you have time.

Portstewart is a sleeping giant, an excellent track. The enormous dunes on the opening holes are about as dramatic as they come. In my opinion, Portstewart should receive a lot more credit than it does. If you can find a bed at Rosemary White's Maddybenny Farm close by, you can look forward to the best breakfast in the world. Would you believe Irish Mist with your porridge? It is like jet fuel, and it will surely put your game into overdrive.

At this stage the Dublin tourists have a choice. You can (1) go into County Donegal and play Rosapenna, an original Old Tom Morris layout built in 1893. Later in life it was modified by James Braid and Harry Vardon. Is there any course anywhere that can claim a link with three such famous men? Or (2) you can go to Ballyliffin, which Nick Faldo unsuccessfully tried to purchase a few years ago.

Faldo said, "This is the most natural golf links I have ever played. I am amazed by the quality, the ruggedness and vastness of the terrain. It is a masterpiece." I take his word for it because I have never been that far north myself yet. I certainly intend to make the trip sometime. Murvagh, halfway between Donegal and Rossnowlagh, has much more to offer than just being the longest course in Ireland at 7,200 yards. You will also experience fine scenery and many interesting holes.

Below are two of the many helpful golf service companies that you can contact before you make your trip to Ireland.

S.W.I.N.G.
Southwest Ireland Golf Ltd.
24 Denny Street,
Tralee, County Kerry
Tel: +353-66-712 5733
E-mail: swing@iol.ie

JD Golf Tours
18 Tullyglass Hill,
Shannon, County Clare
Tel: +353-61-364000
E-mail: jdgolf@iol.ie

⊛

CHAPTER 4

A Personal Miscellany of Irish Golf Holes

Allow me to take you on another tour, this time a personal pot-pourri of fine Irish holes, selected at random, for a myriad of illogical, emotional reasons. The holes selected appear only in the same sequence as they do at home. I also adopted a limit of one hole per course.

1. Royal Portrush, Par 4, 389 yards

Believe it or not, I love the white out-of-bounds fences on *both* sides of this elusive, windswept fairway. While it can be horribly nerve-wrecking to have to face them as the first shot of the day, I like them on account of the way I felt after playing an important interprovincial match for Munster against John Dickson of Ulster in 1982. Dickson holed a beauty from 25 feet on the eighteenth green to square the match, making sudden death play necessary. My opponent promptly sliced his drive from the first (nineteenth) tee over the OB fence. Ever so carefully, I steered an iron shot not very far up the fairway. John reloaded, and to his consternation and my relief, hooked over the other fence on the left. We shook hands there and then, and left the three balls where they lay.

The first shot at Portrush is certainly one for which you will need all of your faculties. It is as worrisome a first shot as I have ever faced. Rushing onto the tee, late, with your laces undone, will cause you to be out of the game before you can shout "Fore!" The second shot is also a daunting one because a very strongly hit iron is needed to reach the elevated green. There is a massive trap on the front left ready to swallow a weak-willed golfer whole. To play this hole well is an excellent confidence-booster for all of the marvellous challenges that lie ahead.

2. County Louth, Par 3, 166 yards

I understand that this hole is now actually the fifth. The order of play has been changed since my last visit. But in my mind it is still the second, the way I remember the course. County Louth (Baltray) has the most wonderful collection of par-three holes, and No. 2 is arguably the best of them. Depending on the wind, anything from a 3-iron to a 9-iron could be the required artillery. The green is narrow, with Ballybunion-like traps and mounds on the right, and gentle, beguiling Lahinch-like swales on the left. To be certain of your par, hit the green, because recovering from either side is no bargain.

3. Killeen Course, Killarney, Par 3, 193 yards

I love par threes. This one is both heavenly scenic and diabolically difficult. You must play across the edge of Lough Leane to a green that is beautifully framed by rhododendron bushes. The tiny hump-backed green sits on a ledge above the lake. It is a shy orphan that rarely embraces "company" and rejects advances in all directions. Anyone who can hit a long iron that lands and stays on this tiny upturned saucer of a green is a player.

4. Cork at Little Island, Par 4, 450 yards

This is a tremendous challenge. The tee shot has to carry more than 200 yards from the back tee over the rugged, rocky edge of the Lee Estuary to reach a fairway that graduates gently uphill to a long, slender, well-trapped green, between rows of colourful gorse. Long, bold, straight hit-

Cork's fourth hole calls for a strong drive across the rocky Lee Estuary. This wobbly swing of mine did not make it. (D.K. Davis)

ting is required. The fifth hole at Cork is equally outstanding, and these two holes (along with Royal County Down's 8th and 9th) could well be the best pair of "back-to-backers" in all of Ireland.

5. The Island, Par 4, 330 yards
The Island Golf Club dates all the way back to 1890. Back then it was predominantly a Protestant club that did not allow play on the sabbath. After a while, some of the Catholic minority decided they did not like this restriction. So they broke away and founded their own club at Portmarnock. In spite of many changes over the years, The Island is still a very natural and traditional-looking links. Justifying its name, the course is actually surrounded on all sides by water, and in the old days the only access was made by boat. Now situated opposite a growing Malahide village, one has to drive on a longish sweep to reach it by a narrow bridge. There are some marvellous holes here, especially the short

thirteenth. But I also love the short, archaic fifth. A drive through a gap in the dunes to a fairway completely enclosed in its own amphitheatre leaves a short iron shot to small green tucked away in a trough surrounded by humps and hollows. This is old style golf that is good for the golfing soul. I still love to walk through a gap, anticipating the result of a blind shot.

The Island and Portstewart are two Irish golf links that are seriously undervalued. It may be because of their proximity to more glamorous and famous sisters — Portmarnock and Portrush, respectively. But if you "dated" the two lesser known ones and missed the "big names," you would not lose out on one iota of beauty and interest.

6. Ballybunion, Par 4, 364 yards

Three hundred and sixty-four yards of "nothing," and yet this is one tough S.O.B. It's especially difficult into the wind, which, fortunately, rarely happens at Ballybunion. (Joke.) This used to be the opening hole. I can still remember my first time standing on that tee with Father Enright and complaining that there was "no fairway!" There is not a single trap or dune on this hole. There is nothing to aim at. You could argue that the fairway is 20 or 150 yards wide, depending on your point of view. The hole appears defenceless. Do not believe it! How wrong you would be. Hit your approach shot one foot off line and it will be carried away to perdition by any one of the many little runoffs at the sides of a slim, elevated green. If Donald Ross had built this one, he would have been really proud of it.

7. Dooks, Par 5, 480 yards

Played in a broad left-to-right sweep from the centre of the course out towards the sea, the seventh at Dooks is a straightforward, "reachable-in-two" par five, provided the wind is not against. Nothing exceptional. Especially when you realize the magnificent deserted beach backdrop is only one of the many beautiful sights on this glorious piece of golfing ground. Dooks is well hidden away and off the beaten track, but it is well worth the effort to find it. The course is an antique and appears pretty easy, but it can jump up and bite you when you least expect it. It can also present a few nineteenth century golfing challenges that you might never have experienced before.

8. East Clare, Par 3, 145 yards

A delightful little hole, worthy of a rustic landscape painting by the noteworthy English artist John Constable. It is played over a small pond to a beautifully positioned green that is set into a hill, and it is framed by deep sculptured bunkers at the front and in back. A large overhanging tree dominates on the left. My friend Dr. Arthur Spring, who took a leaf out of Dr. MacKenzie's book by following a similar career path—going from medicine to golf design—can be proud of the fine holes he created on this little-known jewel of a golf course. East Clare is also off the beaten track, but close by is the scenic Lough Derg, where boating and fishing put golf in the back seat. This remote course is astonishingly only twenty-five miles from Limerick City and the Shannon Airport. John Joyce, who found this formerly inaccessible piece of disused bog land and declared it suitable for golf, is some imaginative genius. But I wish he had stayed with the name I gave the course when we walked it together before a sod was disturbed: Coolreagh Golf Club. I thought that had a soothing ring to it.

9. Royal County Down, Par 4, 458 yards

Without a doubt, this is one of the world's most spectacular holes. A blind tee shot over a large hill will have your ball plunging down into a deep corridor between huge dunes covered in the most fierce looking gorse and scrub. Another giant sand hill is just to the right of the large undulating green. Two deep bunkers are cut into the apron to prevent the run-up entry. There are two other enormous bunkers on the left and right, with the most ferocious looking wild grass growing all over them. When you walk after your tee shot and reach the top of the hill, stop for a brief moment and take in the stunning view: the fairway and green; the clubhouse with its bowling greens behind it; the silver turrets of the Slieve Donard Hotel; the beach and the town of Newcastle. And towering above all are the majestic Mountains of Mourne, sweeping down to the sea. It is simply too much to feast your eyes upon in one sweep. I am not sure if the crusty members of RCD deserve all of this! Unfortunately, it is a bit of an anticlimax to have to set off to play a much inferior looking, but by no means less difficult, back nine.

10. Mullingar, Par 4, 434 yards

One of the famous "Triumvirate," James Braid, built the Mullingar course in the early part of the twentieth century. It was another era, but the course has stood the test of time very well. If it could be stretched just a little, it would break the stoutest of hearts. Mullingar's most interesting feature is its small, well-protected greens. The par-four tenth hole does not need any stretching. It is a converted par five. When I began playing, par was not a word we used at all—it was bogey. The first time I heard the word "par" was on *Shell's Wonderful World of Golf*. When I began golfing at Limerick Golf Club in 1961, "Colonel" Bogey was the accepted standard. It was the Yanks who invented par and decided that a bogey was bad news. At Ballybunion in 1962, the scorecard showed the course rating was "Bogey 76." At Limerick it was 73. Those marks were the measuring sticks. The tenth at Mullingar is such a difficult hole that it could easily fit into the rotation at Medinah. A brave tee shot must be hit over a large tree on the right-hand corner of the fairway. The fairway bends right and then left, and goes up and down as well. It can make you feel seasick. The tee shot that successfully carries over that big tree will eliminate most of these difficulties, and the rest is manageable. But if you fail to get over that tree, or decide to play safe by going left of it, you will have to settle for a "bogey" and forget about matching par.

11. Waterville, Par 5, 500 yards

Whoever named the eleventh hole at Waterville "Tranquillity" had a sense of humour. Five hundred yards of narrow, twisting fairway winds its way through a valley of high dunes, undulations, and bunkers. There is trouble on all sides. The green sits placidly on a knoll, impervious to the trials and tribulations that have to be overcome to reach its sanctuary. The green can just about be reached in two, unless the wind is against. The narrowness of the fairway, however, makes it difficult to lay up. You may as well take a deep breath, go for it, and be rewarded or damned.

12. Tramore, Par 4, 350 yards

Tramore's twelfth hole makes me think briefly that I am at glorious Sunningdale. Parts of this County Waterford course are heathland, parts of it have a links feel, and other parts of it are parkland. It is a most interesting and enjoyable place to play golf. The twelfth hole is short, but the tee shot is tight. At 210 yards from the tee there is a drain or burn that crosses the fairway. It will put a sudden stop to your gallop, if you are an over-hit golf ball. A lovely green, framed by trees and traps, has a nasty step running diagonally through it. You had better be precise with your approach. Before leaving Tramore, do not forget to pay tribute to one of Tramore's favourite sons, the late caddie Rooney. His famous hat is suitably framed and hanging in a place of honour in the men's locker room.

13. Ceann Sibeal (Dingle), Par 5, 560 yards

The British magazine *Golf Monthly* called Ceann Sibeal "a gem off the beaten track." It is also the only course I know where the game is played "as gaelige" (in the Irish language). After all, you are in the heart of the native speaking Gaeltacht. Why not increase the fun, and play golf in "Irish" yourself?

It is also time for a ruling. The dilemma coming up may have you scratching your head. The thirteenth is by far the toughest hole on the course, because a stream crosses the fairway twice. The hole is a sharp dogleg to the right. An OB wall runs all the way along the right-hand side from tee to green, turning sharply right at about 250 yards. Just outside the wall lurks a small but lively stream. Where the wall turns, the water divides in two and one part runs straight on across the fairway. The other part of the stream turns right, still outside the wall, but it enters the field of play in front of the green. All along the left are dunes and rough. Only a madman would try to reach this green in two. This is a complicated hole that once caused a complicated rules conundrum. A player hit his tee shot and his ball went over the out-of-bounds wall and into the stream. The stream was in flood and the ball was carried under the wall and back onto the golf course, about fifty yards upstream. The player claimed that this was a "rub of the green." He picked his ball out of the water, penalized himself one stroke, and played on. Was he correct? Very tricky. Answer: No! Look it up.

14. County Sligo (Rosses Point), Par 4, 433 yards

There are several obstacles at this fine hole. But before tackling them you must first admire the fine view of the Atlantic on the right and the holes to follow stretching out ahead. The tee is set into a large hill well above the landing area. The drive has to carry over a pair of deep, diagonal bunkers to reach a wide fairway. The left-hand side of the fairway requires a longer carry, but playing from there makes the second shot a lot simpler. Going at the green from the right-hand side brings a deceptively wide (but hidden) stream and a series of troublesome dunes near the front right-hand corner into play. A bold shot is needed to make sure of getting over all that stuff, but don't go over the green, either. There is even worse trouble lurking!

15. Mahony's Point, Killarney, Par 4, 252 yards

Every course should have a reachable par four. This one is a favourite—not so much for anything particularly special about the hole, but because of a conversation I overheard there once. The erudite golf commentator Bruce Critchley, as a member of the English golf team, was fighting for his life in a match against one of the old enemy from Scotland. Play was held up, as often happens at a short par four. The contrast between the two players could not have been greater. Bruce, now known to Sky viewers as "the Colonel," was at that time a tall, blond, elegant, bespectacled Englishman. In the other corner was a short, dark, and swarthy Scot who did not remotely resemble officer material. For want of something to say, as they waited for the green to clear, the "braveheart" Scot inquired:

"What do you do to earn a crust, Brucie?"

"I don't work, actually," replied Critchley.

"Weel, ye better getta wirk now. Ye're three doon an' foor t'go!"

16. Carlow, Par 4, 434 yards

All my hopes and dreams died at Carlow's sixteenth hole in the Irish Close Championship of 1978. Having been beaten in the quarterfinals the previous year at Westport, and clearly at the height of my powers, with a number of Scratch Cup victories under my belt, I went down to Carlow full of intent. I came through the qualifying stages with flying colours. At long last, was I beginning to mature and play sensibly? One of the reasons for this overdue state of affairs was that my father insisted that my brother, Dermot, should caddie for me, and that I should follow his course and tactical strategies at all times.

I was told, "Let Dermot make the decisions. You just play golf!"

The plan worked well for four days. I beat three current Internationals in a row, including the man who had beaten me in the last eight the previous year, twice national champion Martin O'Brien. Once more I reached the quarterfinal stage. Eddie Dunne, from Athlone, was the opposition. I was sure I could beat Eddie, too. But my normally accurate iron play started to go off, and I struggled around the lovely

parkland layout, which features some of the smallest greens
in Ireland. Three down at the turn, I received a ferocious
lecture from "The Mouth" (my brother). Responding
immediately, I holed a good birdie putt at No.10 and suddenly I was off and running. I had gone ahead by the time
we reached the fifteenth, but I faltered again. All flat and
three to go. The sixteenth at Carlow is a tough uphill hole
through a saddle of gentle hills. Its small green is half hidden at the foot of another large hill that is covered with
trees. Eddie snap-hooked his tee shot. I got such a fright
that I sliced mine wildly to the right, but I was not too badly
positioned on top of a hill with a clear view. My opponent
could only lay up. I swear I wanted to do likewise, because
I thought the green was out of reach, but Dermot insisted:
"This is it. This is your chance. Go for the juggler. Faint
heart never won anything!"

The driver was forced into my hands. I stone cold
topped the ball up against a tree and I was dead. A relieved
Eddie Dunne made a killer birdie two at the next and I was
history. My woes increased the following year when the
championship went to one of my favourite haunts,
Ballybunion, where I have hardly ever lost a match over the
years. But nine weeks before the championship, I fell and
broke my arm. I never got another chance.

17. The European Club, Par 4, 392 yards

What you have here is a dramatic hole on a wonderful golf
course that has many exciting features. No. 17 plays down
into a deep valley surrounded by huge dunes on both sides.
Mountains, sea, bracken, and sand form a backdrop that rivals
Royal County Down's ninth for being the best-looking hole
in Ireland. The fairway appears narrow, but it is actually
sixty yards wide. Three skinny thorn bushes in the middle
of the driving area cause havoc in the mind's eye. The green
is set on a lovely table surrounded by dunes—perfect for
spectators on a fine sunny afternoon. The hole is named
after Sir Henry Cotton. He could not have a finer epitaph.

18. Adare, Par 5, 525 yards

This is one of the last golf holes designed by one of the game's greatest architects, the late Robert Trent Jones Sr. When he was introducing it to the members of the Irish media, he called it "the best finishing par-five hole in golf." Having failed to negotiate it safely many times, I have no reason to dispute that claim. Its perceived difficulty is only increased on account of an incident in December of 1999, when I had to rescue my brother Dermot from drowning. He fell into the free-flowing Maigue River—which runs right beside the fairway and in front of the green—when the riverbank gave way under him as he took up his stance. Fortunately, he hit some solid ground and the water only reached his shoulders. What a dramatic moment that was! Lee Harrington and I managed to get him out safely. Dermot changed his clothes and finished the hole, registering one of the greatest pars I have ever seen. Since then I have been heavily criticized by quite a few of his so-called friends for not leaving him in the river. Thinking back to the bad advice he gave me at Carlow in 1978 (and some other painful incidents), perhaps I should have done so.

Adare Manor provides a magnificent backdrop for the 18th hole at Adare Golf Club. The river is in play all the way from the tee to the green.

⊛

CHAPTER 5

Tiger O'Woods and the Sundance Kid

A golfing itch afflicts the billionaire Limerick-born horse owner and international financier J.P. McManus every five years. In 1990, he conceived the idea of sponsoring and running a Pro-Am Golf Classic at his home course, Limerick Golf Club, to raise much-needed funds for local charities. It was a roaring success. Many of the top players from the European Tour turned up to enjoy a wonderful two days of innovative hospitality. Although J.P. invited his wealthy friends to pay a fat fee for the privilege of playing, local golfers were not excluded. They were offered the chance of taking part by prequalifying through less expensive satellite events. All of this activity in various golf clubs throughout the midwest of Ireland multiplied the receipts to around IR£2 million.

Then, in 1995, using the same formula, J.P. managed to woo three stars from the U.S. Senior circuit to join the European Tour players, who did not need much persuading to return to Limerick to help repeat the success of five years earlier. The Americans were Jim Colbert, Bob Murphy, and Tom Wargo. This time IR£3 million was raised, mainly due to a highly successful auction during the Gala Ball that was held on the final night of the tournament. IR£3 million is a very considerable sum when dis-

Tiger Woods checks the clothing brand of the Sundance Kid (J.P. McManus) at the 2000 Pro–Am Classic. (Limerick Leader)

tributed in a place the size of Limerick (approximately 100,000 souls). I had the illuminating experience of caddieing for Murphy, against whom I competed in college events in Florida in 1965. That information sure surprised him!

Payne Stewart was a vital catalyst in the planning of the millennium 2000 event. During his visit to Waterville prior to the 1999 Open, Payne encouraged a dithering J.P. to "go for it" one more time.

"It sounds like a lot of fun," Stewart told him. "I will definitely come over myself, and I am sure I will be able to persuade a few of the Isleworth gang to come over a couple days early on their way to the 2000 Open at St. Andrews. Together we can turn it into one of the most successful charity events of its type ever."

The Isleworth golf/residential community in Orlando, Florida is positively dripping with stars of the U.S. PGA Tour, most notably Tiger Woods and Mark O'Meara. Mr. McManus was an established resident of that exclusive complex long before any of the golf stars arrived. His locker is side by side with a Mr. T. Woods, so they know each other quite well. When J.P. met Payne and Tiger at the 1999 Ryder Cup, the 2000 Pro-Am was discussed.

"Are you inviting me?" Tiger asked, who earlier that summer had spent a very enjoyable week in Ireland with O'Meara, Jantzen, and Stewart as J.P.'s guests while preparing for the 1999 British Open at Carnoustie. J.P., using some typical soft-sell psychology, said no more than, "You will be made very welcome if you do come." It was left to the "Chief Recruiting Officer" (Payne) to do the rest. How well he succeeded. But more about that anon. I must first tell you a little of the background of J.P. McManus.

Back in the 1960s there was a young, fresh-faced bulldozer driver employed by his earth moving contractor father, Johnny. He was the smallest and youngest in a fairly tough crew, who worked, played, and drank hard. The kid was hurling mad, but he did not have the outstanding athleticism needed to achieve his sporting dreams like his boyhood pals, Joe McKenna, Eamonn Grimes, and Pat Hartigan. All three of these youngsters went on to win the All-Ireland Hurling Championship with Limerick in 1973.

At lunchtime his work colleagues used to send the young fellow to the nearest bookie's office to place their bets on the day's horse races. Our young friend was pretty sharp. He did not take long to figure out that his "elders and betters" hardly ever picked a winner, so he secretly began carrying their bets and developed an interest in studying "the form" for himself. Using his colleagues' money to make his own far more successful wagers, it was not long before his flair and ability opened up new opportunities, as soon as he accumulated a little war chest. He applied for, and was granted, a bookmaker's licence. After a while he realized that a bookmaker "had to bet" on every race, whereas the punter could pick and choose. He preferred the latter. Showing no fear, he began placing carefully researched larger and larger bets. He was extraordinarily successful. Because of his gunslinger coolness he became known as "The Sundance Kid," after the Robert Redford character in the movie *Butch Cassidy and the Sundance Kid*. His reputation grew. The Irish and English bookmaking fraternities became scared stiff of him and refused to carry his bets anymore. Stories of IR£1 million wagers are the stuff of legend, but the man himself will not confirm or deny any of it. He intimates that a lot of this talk is speculative nonsense because "the best strokes have never been told because they might have to be used again." Forced to go further afield, J.P. looked for new forms of endeavour that would yield big dividends. Operating from his home in County Limerick, McManus quickly became a millionaire making "spread bets" on American football games by telephone. The discovery of the ability to be able do this had more to do with a unique mathematical brain than his scanty knowledge of the NFL. He calculated the odds and permutations in his head as effectively as any expensive high-tech computer. From his present-day Switzerland base, J.P. now uses that same brain as one of the world's biggest and most successful players in the international currency markets. He has a private jet "for getting around more efficiently" and owns the exclusive Sandy Lane Hotel and Golf Complex in Barbados, as well a share in the Isleworth Estate in Orlando, Florida.

Professional golfers are particularly impressed by individual success stories because they are so self-reliant themselves. Because of his residence at Isleworth, McManus has many friends among the stars of the PGA Tour, and several of them make regular trips to Ireland as his guests to play "private golf."

In spite of all of his exposure to fame and fortune, J.P. has remained a modest, "ordinary" fellow with the same schoolboy chums with whom he grew up. You could quite easily run into him playing a friendly but highly competitive golf match off his fifteen handicap for "a couple of shillings" with McKenna, Grimes, and Hartigan at Limerick,

Lahinch, or Waterville, where he is a member.

The members of Limerick Golf Club were, to say the least, skeptical and disbelieving when they began hearing rumours about what J.P. was planning for his year 2000 event and who was coming to the third edition of the J.P. McManus Classic. Large pinches of salt were being liberally used in the bar of the modest clubhouse.

"Tiger is coming!"

"Arra, go way outa dat!"

"Duval is coming!"

"Will you stop your codding!"

"Jantzen is coming!"

"Gimme a break!"

"Mediate, Appleby, and Allenby are all coming"

"Feck off! Pull the other one!"

"Mark O'Meara is coming!"

"I suppose he has to come to keep an eye on Tiger. Ha, ha!"

Not to mention any of the star players from Europe whose names kept cropping up. It was too good to be true. But it was true!

The atmosphere of expectation at Ballyclough on Monday, July 10, 2000 was extraordinary and unforgettable. Tiger & Co. had arrived earlier that morning in Shannon, having flown through the night. They had completed the Western Open in Chicago the previous afternoon. With perfect timing, Robert Allenby was the winner of that one. After three hours of what could only have been a fitful rest at the Adare Manor Hotel, they were whisked by helicopter to the course and rapturously greeted by a crowd that was strictly limited to 8,000 privileged spectators. On arrival, Tiger said, "I am feeling a bit sleepy but I am sure I will be okay once we start playing." He should play in a "half-sleep" more often, because he put on the most incredible display of shot-making on the short (6,525 yards), tight, wind-swept, tree-lined layout. His ball control was incredible and all done with style and ease—as if I did not know already there was talent to burn in his fingertips.

Tiger and his "chaperone" (the author).

Here was proof yet again that "nothing succeeds like excess." Later he told the "gentlemen of the media" that he was practicing his low trajectory shots for the Open Championship. The fact that he shot 64 and broke the long-standing course record by three strokes was almost a forgotten detail. What impressed us the most was the grace and good humour of the guy. He spoke pleasantly to everybody and anybody. What had happened to that aggressive, fist-waving lunatic we had seen on TV?, I wondered.

On Tuesday I was assigned to "chaperone" Ronan Rafferty and his team of three Ballyclough members, the Quane brothers. My services were superfluous in that company, I can assure you. Suddenly, out of the blue, I was called off the course and asked to report to the Chief Starter.

"Would you be prepared to walk around with Tiger this

afternoon and keep score for him and his team?"

"You're kidding?"

"No."

"Would I what?!"

"Be on the tee fifteen minutes before time and make sure you fill out the card in full, and get it signed and returned to the PGA Office as soon as possible after play."

I could not believe my luck. I learned later that my friend and protégé, the Limerick club professional Lee Harrington, who was caddieing for Tiger, had put in a special request that I should be allowed to go around with them inside the ropes. Apparently there had been a "minor mix-up" with the card on the previous day and Lee wanted no more slipups. It would have been impossible not to feel slightly nervous waiting for the world's number one golfer to show up. How would he react to a new face in his entourage? When he eventually arrived on the tee, he walked straight past me to the front of the tee and greeted a young boy in a wheelchair. Obviously he had been tipped off about the presence of the lad. He came back and did a few stretches while I asked the amateurs for their handicaps and made sure I knew who was who. When I asked Tiger for his handicap he smiled broadly and I relaxed. The paparazzi took over and began taking group pictures. Lee invited me to stand in, too. I said to Tiger, "Sorry about this, Tiger. You must be sick of photographs."

"No problem," he replied. "I will stay here all day for photographs. Just do not ask me to sign anything!" That put to rest my plans of having him sign the five caps I had with me belonging to family and friends. Earlier we had been asked to shield Tiger from any possible autograph seekers, but I thought he might just make an odd exception. There was finality in his voice so I did not dare ask. Having walked a golf course with him, I can now understand why. If he stopped for just one autograph signing, there would have been pandemonium.

Playing with Tiger were three fellows who had won the

Marie at the J.P. McManus Pro–Am Classic. (Tony Rodgers)

qualifier at Nenagh Golf Club in nearby County Tipperary.
One was nine time Irish Champion jockey Christy Roche,
a five-foot-nothing with Popeye arms, playing off eleven.
Christy could drive it with any scratch man right-handed,
but his left-handed putting was dire! Another was Tom
Harty, a twelve handicap Tipperary farmer, who was wearing his short-sleeved yellow shirt daringly unbuttoned and
an incongruous black woollen ski hat over his Mick Jagger
1970s hair style. How he could have worn that headgear in
the warm sun, I do not know. But boy, was he a cool one
underneath. Straight off, he and Tiger had the winks, nods,
and banter going. Tiger had effortlessly switched onto the
Irish way of "slagging," and he certainly gave the impression he was there for a laugh rather than a serious round of
golf with a big prize to be won.

The third man was eighteen-year-old Kieran McManus,
a fifteen handicapper and J.P.'s son. Kieran told me he had
to prequalify just like everybody else and that he "hardly
ever" plays—"too much studying to do." After watching
him perform, I do not believe a bit of it! This young man is
an uncut golfing diamond.

Just before a ball was struck the crowd shouted at us hangers-on to "Get down!" so that they could see more clearly. So we all ducked down onto our hunkers, including Tiger. That got a big laugh. It was not the time or the place to ask Tiger for the secrets of his success, but as we went around I managed to have a few little interchanges with him. On the third tee, I asked him about Butch Harmon's input.

"He kicks my butt, morning 'til night—but I like that," said Tiger.

So now we know Tiger is a masochist. He listened with wide-eyed curiosity when I told him about the Alister MacKenzie connection with the Ballyclough course and that Walter Hagen had been a visitor in 1937. We had a long delay on the fourth tee. Tiger seemed to be curious about Tom Harty's wooden-headed three-wood. It had a bamboo-like flex in the shaft, but Tom was launching some pretty impressive tee shots with it. Tiger asked Tom could he waggle it. As Tiger amused himself with the suppleness of the shaft and the neglected look of the paintless wood, Tom pulled Tiger's driver out of his bag and gave it a fierce swish.

"Do you want to try it, Tom?" Tiger asked.

"I bet you a pound that if I use yours and you use mine, I will outdrive you," challenged the ever bashful and shy Tom Harty.

"I don't know about that, but you are on," replied the Tiger.

Tom went first and hit a screamer that would have been close enough to one of Tiger's more modest efforts. Tiger found the bend in the shaft of Tom's club too much and he mistimed the strike. The ball hooked and only flew two hundred yards or so. A clear win for Harty! Then Tiger turned away, feigning anger, and pretended to throw the offending club into the nearby bushes, saying, "This is no good, no good at all." I got in on the act by saying, "If Tom owned Tiger's clubs he might be the world's Number One. It is the arrow after all, not the Indian." That got a good conversation going on equipment and a bit of swing theory. Tiger emphasised the importance of connecting the swing

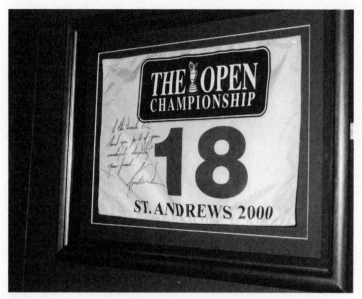

A signed gift from Tiger following his victory at the 2000 Open Championship. "To the Limerick GC. Thank you for all your wonderful hospitality—Tiger Woods." (Cliodhna McGill)

of the arms to the body so that everything moved together. Somebody asked him how he achieved such consistency. "Hit the ball one way all the time, unless you absolutely have to go the other way. Play whichever way is most comfortable to your eye and the way you see the shots." I see everything right-to-left, but Tiger clearly is a left-to-right man.

Limerick Centenary Captain Terry Clancy was stewarding at No. 17 in the vicinity of where Tiger's ball landed. When the maestro arrived, Terry said, "I teed it up for you, Tiger."

Tiger, quick as flash, took a tee out his pocket, handed it to Terry, and retorted, "Do a better job of it next time."

We wonder at the man's great length, but I was more or less expecting that. Up close I was even more impressed by his control of distance and trajectory. There is no doubt that he was practicing the latter all the time he was at

Ballyclough, getting ready for the challenge of St. Andrews the following week. He was only bunting the ball forward most of the time, using a restricted, cut-off swing. Only once or twice did he cut loose and go full throttle.

On the eighth tee, Tiger asked me how many Stableford points the team had scored at the previous hole. "Tree," I answered in my flat Limerick brogue.

"You mean we have just gone tree, tree, tree?" said Tiger, the mimic.

That got a huge guffaw. He was learning the Limerick accent and knew how to take the Mickey, too! I gave him a stern impromptu lecture on Irish history, telling him to be careful.

"The Irish had always managed to overcome their invaders with kindness," I explained, "eventually inducing them to become more Irish than the Irish themselves. If you continue to speak in such a manner, you will soon qualify to be an honorary Irishman, and be rechristened Tiger O'Woods!"

⊛
Chapter 6

Payne Stewart's Irish Legacy

"Hey, what's that y'all are doin'?" the stranger asked. "Sure looks like fun. Can I come down and join y'all?"

Limerick and Ballybunion Golf Club members Basil Patterson and his late, lamented wife Betty, two extremely keen, but by no means expert players, were practising their putting before dinner at the Hotel Europe during the 1991 Irish Open at Killarney when they were startled by a high-pitched Missouri twang from an upstairs window. Not having a clue who the heckler was, they barely acknowledged him and carried on with their private game of trying to relieve one another of the fifty pence side wager for which they were playing. Imagine their surprise a few moments later when the newly crowned U.S. Open champion, Payne Stewart, joined them. At first they did not recognize him because he was "in disguise"—no trademark knickers, no flamboyant shirt, and no cap. He borrowed Basil's putter and challenged Betty. Round and around they went on the rough and ready makeshift putting green in the hotel car park, until Payne finally engineered it that Betty would win. Then, "materialising" a box of golf balls, magician style, from his person, he presented it to his two new Irish friends.

That is typical of how Payne Stewart introduced himself to Ireland, and he continued behaving in such fashion until

July, 1998. The late, lamented Payne Stewart drives off the first tee at Ballybunion. Watching from the left are Tiger Woods and Mark O'Meara. On the right (in sunglasses) is J.P. McManus. (Damian Breathnach)

his final visit in 1999. It must be said his friendliness was reciprocated while his privacy was respected, too. Payne made an instant hit with the Irish. During the same tournament, Marie and I were in our favourite restaurant—Foley's on Main Street in downtown Killarney—when Payne and his entourage entered. Quite spontaneously, everyone stood up and applauded him. He was slightly taken aback, but once he sat down nobody bothered him or approached his table. He was allowed to be "one of us." The diners were content to sup under the same roof as the current U.S. Open champion.

Payne became very fond of his regular pre–British Open trips to Ireland. He made Waterville his base and blended in well with the locals, joining in their pub singsongs and enthralling them with virtuoso performances on one of the ten mouth organs he always carried with him. He was a natural in the ambience of Irish pub life, and he was loved for it—so much so that it was announced during the Ryder Cup at Brookline, only a few weeks before he was tragically and bizarrely killed, that he had been elected Honorary Captain of Waterville Golf Club for the millennium year 2000. It is a shame he did not live to enjoy a few visits to Waterville in this honorary capacity, because the "craic" would have been mighty.[1] What a Captain's Dinner he would have hosted!

1999 was a strange golfing year. Stewart's U.S. Open win at "Paynehurst" was the best tournament I ever saw on television. The course and the play of both winner and runner-up, Phil Mickelson ("Fickelson," I call him[2]), was quite majestic all week long, and Tiger was in the thick of it, too. The patience, self-control, and fortitude shown by Stewart was outstanding—particularly the way he played the seventy-second hole. It took great guts, presence of mind, and self-belief to lay up the way he did, with the whole world watching.

The 1999 British Open, only a few weeks later, was one of the worst spectacles I ever had to endure in forty years of watching championship golf. It was ruined by a course that reduced everyone, except Paul Lawrie, to idiot status.

Payne was the first American to accept J.P. McManus's invitation to his Pro-Am at Limerick in 2000, but unfortunately a runaway plane took care of that.

When the J.P. McManus Pro-Am at Limerick raised the unbelievable sum of IR£12 million ($14 million), much of the credit rightly went to Stewart. It was he who gave JP the final push to go ahead by promising that he would not only come himself but would lean on his buddies—Tiger, Mark, David, Stuart, Bob, Lee, and Rocco—to come, too.

When Payne died so tragically, it became almost a mission for his pals not to renege on their promise. Then Waterville Golf Club decided to commemorate Payne by erecting a bronze statue in honour of their Honorary Millennium Captain. The unveiling was arranged to coincide with the Pro-Am, and it all worked out so well. Payne, I am sure, smiled down from heaven knowing that he was a big part, helping

July, 2000. Payne's widow, Tracey, Tiger Woods and Mark O'Meara attend the unveiling of a statue in memory of the former U.S. Open champion at Waterville GC. (Courtesy of Allsport)

to raise such a huge sum for very worthy causes.

I am sure you will wonder how a little Pro-Am at Limerick, a town of 100,000 souls, could raise so much through a golf tournament.

This is how it happened.

First, J.P. McManus put up the purse (£400,000) and covered all expenses out of his own pocket. About a dozen qualifying tournaments with an entry fee of £1,000 per team were held all over the North Munster area in advance. An average of perhaps £50,000 per venue was gathered that way. There was a mini-tented village selling golf equipment, memorabilia, and souvenirs. An admission fee of £20 per day was charged of perhaps 8,000 spectators. Limerick Golf Club provided its course free of charge for the event, and the members more or less exclusively provided all the necessary volunteers. None of the players accepted a penny of their prize money. It was all thrown back into the pot.

But the real money-spinner was the Grand Auction and Gala Ball at Adare Manor. What transpired there was mind-boggling! After the most exquisite meal and fine wines,[3] some of the richest people in the world vied with each other to throw their money away in reckless fashion, buying items that on face value were not worth a fraction of what they paid for them. It was simply a case of off-loading a million here and a million there so that less fortunate people might have a more comfortable and satisfying life — sentiments that we all agree with and that were certainly encouraged by J.P.'s warm-up speech.

Amongst the Items That Sold and for How Much

Saddlers Wells Horse Breeding Nomination: £360,000. Kiawah Island Ryder Cup Flag (signed by teams): £25,000. Two debenture tickets for Wimbledon 2001: £70,000. Payne Stewart Portrait by Peter Deighan: £1.4 million. A specially commissioned piece of Waterford Crystal: £50,000. A painting by one of Ireland's greatest artists, Jack B. Yeats: £1 million (this item was actually a good value!). Four exclusive tickets to any Manchester United Champions League home game: £25,000. A Peter Curling Cartoon of various characters who took part in the Pro-Am: £1.1 million (the focus of the picture was a clearly reluctant Tiger dressed as a jockey and about to be forcibly mounted on Istabraq, Mr. J.P. McManus's famous champion horse, to race against an already mounted Dermot Desmond, an Irish business tycoon riding a donkey). A round of golf with Tiger Woods and Mark O'Meara at Isleworth: £1.4 million (when O'Meara saw the bidding for this one rise beyond belief, he interjected that he would throw in a free lesson and some food as well). A flag personalised by Tiger from the 2000 U.S. Open at Pebble Beach: £1 million. David Duval's scorecard from the 1999 Bob Hope Classic when he shot 59: £14,000. Tickets and accommodation for the 2001 Ryder Cup matches: £40,000.

And that was not all of it. When all receipts were added up they came to just under a breathtaking IR£12 million.

1 Craic is a well-known Gaelic colloquialism for fun.

2 For a long time, I have always referred to Phil Mickelson as "Fickleson." It is primarily a play on his given and surnames, but it is also on account of a rather rash statement he made during the 1991 Walker Cup matches at Portmarnock. Phil mused out loud about how ugly the Irish women in his gallery were. A rather rash, foolish, and, dare I say, ill-informed comment that was surely a "throw-away" remark that did not account for the arctic conditions prevailing. Unfortunately it was blown out of proportion in the Irish newspapers the following day. After a hasty retraction and the reasonable claim that he was "misquoted," all was forgiven, but I have referred to Phil as "Fickleson" ever since.

3 Diners at the banquet partook in a seven-course meal that started with smoked chicken together with a crisp summer salad, mustard seed dressing, and watermelon. The second course was a tempura of Berehaven prawns with a sauce gribiche, and peach sorbet with blackberry compote. The main course consisted of roast rack of Adare lamb, pine nuts, and basil galette, mint and basil jus, fresh seasonal vegetables, and new potatoes. Dessert was summer berry tiramisu with raspberry vinaigrette and pistachio ice cream. It was all finished off with freshly brewed tea and coffee, petit fours, and Irish cheeses. Libations were Puligny Montrachet 1997, Chateau Haut Brion 1986, and liqueurs.

✺

CHAPTER 7

Caddie Travels and Travails

"'Tis like this, sir. When my American friends come over here, I caddies for them. When I goes over to America, they caddies for me."

That perfectly reasonable explanation was offered by a beleaguered Lahinch caddie when he was confronted "red-handed" by an investigator from the Tax Authority a few years ago. The taxman wanted to know how the caddie could justify continuing to draw the dole and return "nil" income from his on-course activities, after he saw him carrying the bag of an American visitor at Lahinch.

Every golfer knows that caddies can be eccentric and colourful. I have had the "pleasure" of hiring some rather extraordinary characters to carry my bag around the golf courses of Ireland from time to time. One of the most memorable is the vastly experienced, much travelled John O'Reilly. John worked for touring professional Des Smyth for many years until a serious back injury put a stop to his gallop. While he was recovering and waiting for Padraig Harrington to pop the question, I met him at the 1995 J.P. McManus Pro–Am and told him that my cousin, Roland Stafford, was looking for "a good man" to steer him around Royal Portrush in the British Seniors Open a few weeks later. A deal was done there and then. Roland and John gelled

Irish touring professional Padraig Harrington and caddie John O'Reilly

well and Roland finished a respectable 18th. After the tournament John asked me for a lift back to Dublin and then
more than paid his fare home by recounting a series of the
most incredible stories, which are worth a book of their own.

"I was caddieing for Peter Townsend one season," John
told me. "Peter used to pay me an agreed retainer a week in
advance and then a percentage of his purse at the end of the
tournament. The next tournament was in Berlin. Myself
and three other caddies travelled across to Liverpool on the
ferry, but there was a blackjack game on the boat and I lost
all me money. I still had to get to Berlin but I hadn't a penny.

"We arrive in Liverpool, and I get on the train to
Southampton. The ticket collector was getting too close
for comfort so I knock on a toilet door and shout, 'Tickets!'
The poor guy inside shoves his ticket under the door. That
got me to Southampton. Now we have to catch the ferry to
Holland. One of my caddie friends gets on the boat and
then makes an excuse that he has to get off again. They give

him a pass. He gives it to me and I am on the ferry. In Holland we have to catch a train to Berlin. The lads put me into a golf bag travel cover and lifted me up onto the overhead rack. I was up there for hours without even a drink of water. To get to our destination in Berlin, our train had to briefly go through the Communist sector. The 'Gestapo' came around to stamp the passports. When they had passed by, I jumps out of the bag, gets me passport, borrows a ticket and runs after one of the guards and say, 'You forgot to stamp me passport, sir!' Your man looks at me funny but he stamps me card. I've made it. I'm in Berlin. Townsend has a good week, I make a nice bonus, and I travel home in style.

"When the World Cup was played in Cape Town, it was my first time in Africa. I met a big black African caddie called Jumbo. Huge he was. We became pals. 'I'll look after you, John,' says Jumbo. 'Right,' says I. We went out drinking together. Down the shanty town he brings me to a place called 'The Hole in the Wall.' I am the only white guy in the place. They are all looking at me. Jumbo is there standing beside me and he tells me not to worry he will look after me. Even when I go to the toilet he comes with me. There was a Karaoke going on. They got me up to sing. So I stand there in front of all those black fellas and I say, 'I want to dedicate my song to Nelson Mandela.' The place breaks up with the cheering and the clapping, so I gave them a rousing version of *My Way*. After that, I am home free. They call me Irish Johnny, and for the rest of the week I do not have to put my hand in my pocket to buy another drink.

"So we are on the practice ground at the weekend and big Ernie Els walks up to me. 'Reilly, were you in "The Hole" last night?'

"'I was there the last three nights,' says I.

"He says, 'I would not go within a hundred miles of that place. It is the most dangerous pub in all of Africa!'

"'You couldn't go there with your accent,' says I to Ernie, 'but with my accent I am an honorary member of "The

Hole." Anyway, I am all right: I've got Jumbo to mind me!'"

Now I want you to know that John O'Reilly is no "spring chicken," and he has six grown children scattered around the globe. He is the gentlest of souls with the most wonderful lived-in face and twinkling Irish eyes. You could not help but like him. But his mode of travelling from one tournament to the next is unorthodox to say the least. He had quite a marathon in 1998, beginning at the Sarazen World Open in Georgia. (What a misnomer that is, by the way.)

John was the author of his own problems. On a whim after "the Sarazen," he decided to fly from Atlanta to San Francisco to see his son. Complications arose because before leaving London, John had purchased two tickets. First, a return ticket from London Heathrow to Atlanta. Second, a ticket from London Gatwick to Los Angeles and then onward to Auckland, New Zealand for the World Cup.

When he was in San Francisco, Johnny realized he was already halfway to New Zealand. He phoned his friendly, helpful airline to inquire if he could drive down to L.A. and meet his plane there. Sounds reasonable, but the airline was having none of it. "You must pick up your ticket in London," he was told, "or else pay a $2,000 penalty."

Good grief. You may as well shoot a man as frighten the life out of him!

Johnny flew back to Atlanta, then to Heathrow, caught a train across London to Gatwick, waited several hours, caught a plane back to Atlanta, waited another few hours, and caught his connection to L.A. as originally planned. There, he waited another two or three hours before at last being on his way on a twelve-hour flight to Auckland. All in all that added up to 44 hours of nonstop travel, across so many time zones the mind boggles. Only Johnny O'Reilly could do it. Anybody else would be comatose. Somehow I doubt if John's mental arithmetic was reliable that week. I am sure Harrington did his own adding and subtracting.

On another occasion John's brain was clearly in top gear. It was at Kiawah Island during the 1997 World Cup of Golf.

Padraig Harrington and Paul McGinley won for Ireland and O'Reilly was on Harrington's bag.

Kiawah is a fairly inaccessible place. It is "out in the boondocks," as they say, in the middle of a saltwater swamp about ten miles from Charleston, South Carolina. Getting to and from the course was a nightmare for the caddies during the practice rounds. Something drastic had to be done. Then "Irish Johnny" had a bright idea. He approached the Tournament Director's office and introduced himself as "the head coach of the Irish team," and politely requested a courtesy car. He got it! Now he was able to get to and from the course in comfort. He filled the car with his caddie friends, and they enjoyed waving to the fans, and even signing autographs when they were held up by the daily chaos on the causeway to the course. The World Cup of Golf being what it is, they got away with it. Nobody had heard of these players or the country they represented: Tir na nOg.[1]

My favourite caddie by some distance was my boyhood and lifelong friend, the late James Carew. James was an excellent and highly competitive player himself, which meant he was not always available to be my "minder." That is what he was, too, pouring oil on troubled waters or clearing the red mist were his specialities. It was certain that when James was on the bag one of us at least would stay cool, calm, and collected. And no prizes for guessing who. James had the cunning Irishman's knack of answering a question with another question. A brilliant tactic under fire, because it helped one to concentrate the mind on the consequences of one's actions. James and I were regular golf partners for nearly forty years. It was a terrible blow when he died unexpectedly in 1998, a week before his 52nd birthday.

My youngest brother, Dermot, could be an inspirational and aggravating advisor. He helped me to raise my game to great heights or plumb the depths simultaneously. We saw things differently too often, barely avoiding fisticuffs over golf decisions at times. But if anybody outside the family circle dared criticise either one of us, they were in danger of a severe backlash!

Jim Cleary, from Miltown-Malbay, near Lahinch, was a big warmhearted bagman of mine. His dedication and good humour were a tremendous source of strength to me at the West of Ireland at Rosses Point year after year, often in some of the most vile playing conditions imaginable. The wind and the hailstones never bothered him. We had a few good runs at trying to win the championship together. Much to his chagrin, the severity of the weather finally got the better of me, and after fifteen years of hardship I finally carried out my annual threat "not to come back ever again."

There was a caddie at Tramore called "The Rooney." Note the significant "The". The Tramore members never called him by anything less. He took a shine to me because he seemed to admire my swing and thought I could be the

The late caddie from Tramore GC, "The Rooney." His famous hat hangs today in a special place in the men's locker room.

winner of the big 72-hole Annual Scratch Cup at Tramore. I let him down. One year we led after 63 holes but I collapsed like a cheap suitcase over the final nine holes. All those marathon training sessions with Father Enright could not save me. Amazingly, The Rooney never spoke a word to me, or anybody else — on or off the course. All communication was done through signs and gestures. I know he was not a mute because I was shocked to hear him singing sweetly in the locker room after a few "scoops" during a fog delay. The Rooney was a connoisseur of the golf swing and secretly coached generations of young players behind the club-house and out of sight of the pro. The kids followed him around like the Pied Piper. They were not only mesmerised by his trick shots, but also by his ability to entice the birds and rabbits to take food from his hand. He was that gentle. He could replicate any swing he saw and would demon-strate faults and offer correction without ever uttering a word. It was all done with animated grunts and gestures. Sadly, he came from a tragic family background, never went to school, and was completely illiterate. Still, he was a lovely, warm, kind, and talented person who had eyes that could light up a room. In different circumstances he might have been a substantial professional player, but his back-ground never afforded him the opportunity.

The Cork philosopher Michael Dorgan was about as eccentric a caddie as I ever encountered. A one-time med-ical student who dropped out of college, he was highly articulate and intelligent. He turned up unannounced at courses all over Ireland trying to scrape a few shillings to keep body and soul together. He always seemed to have a newspaper sticking out of his back pocket. He was fanati-cal about solving the daily crossword puzzle. If it were not completed before teeing off, the newspaper would con-tinue to be produced out on the course at every available opportunity. All and sundry would be recruited to assist in solving the more elusive clues. Whenever I gave him a lift home after the golf, our discussions were of politics and philosophy rather than of missed chances, Nicklaus, Palmer, or Player. I understand Michael is still going strong at Royal Dublin and other venues, but I have not seen him for many years.

I had a brief and stormy relationship with a famous caddie at Portmarnock named Peter Maguire. Peter was incorrigible. As far as he was concerned, *he* was the boss. If you doubted his instructions, you might be threatened as follows: "Listen, Boss, if you reach the green with that club, I will take off my trousers and hang them from the clubhouse flagpole." Peter was a superb reader of the Portmarnock greens and I profited from this to great effect. I never had to bother looking at the breaks on the greens myself. I left it entirely to Peter. Unfortunately, I could not cope with his high remunerative expectations and we parted company. Peter used to caddie regularly for a United States senator. This politician loved to get away from it all and play alone with only Peter by his side. One blisteringly hot, summer day the senator found himself in the deep bunker in front of the fourteenth green. Like poor Yorrick in *Hamlet*, the senator could not extricate himself from his sandy grave.

"Ah, Jayzus, sir, ger oura dat bunker an' I'll show you how to do it!" says the bold Maguire.

Without taking off his ever present, heavy, woolen jacket, Peter entered the bunker. Ten swipes later the ball was still at his feet, below ground. Clambering back out, perspiration pouring out of him, he declared, "Now sir, I hope you were able to see what you were doing wrong."

Peter was not famous for his patience and tolerance. These scarce attributes were sorely tested on one particular St. Stephen's Day (Boxing Day) by one of his regular employers at Portmarnock. The member had received the present of a battery-operated caddie car from his wife for Christmas. Turning up for his usual game, he politely told Peter his services would no longer be required. Peter was horrified. He had always carried two bags in this fourball, and now his income was going to be cut in half. At the dogleg third hole, playing directly into the low winter sun, the owner of the new caddie car hit a quick hook into the dunes.

"Did anybody see my ball?"

"No."

"Did you see my ball, Peter?"

"Ask the shaggin' caddie car!"

Caddies are the salts of the earth. They nearly always have improved my enjoyment and ability to score. If I were ever to become wealthy, my caddie would be one of the first with whom I would share my good fortune.

1 Tir na nOg is a mythical island off the West Coast of Ireland where nobody grows old!

⊛

Chapter 8

Ballybunion G.C.
Rags to riches in twenty years

When I began playing at Ballybunion in 1962, the best player in the club was Kieran Allen. He was a long hitter capable of overpowering the course. Unfortunately he emigrated to England in order to earn a living, and was lost to the game in Ireland. Kieran's younger brother Reggie was almost as good, but he too took the emmigrant boat. Bill Harnett was another very good player back then. Bill was a shrewd theorist with a steady, tidy tee-to-green game. However, putting was a bit of a mystery to him and he went side-saddle long before Sam Snead, and then to the long putter, which, in my opinion, should never have been allowed to happen by the powers that be. That long putter is just not golf. Bill set the course record (69) in 1959 and held it proudly until Pat Mulcare and yours truly lowered the mark to 67 in the mid-1970s. Bill Harnett was not in Allen or Mulcare's class, but he was far more "colourful." There are several amusing stories about him, which are worth repeating.

One day while playing a match for the club, Bill was afflicted by a bad nosebleed at the farthest regions of the course. He tried in vain to stop the flow, but to no avail, so he stuck a handful of grass stalks up his nose and battled

The 10th green at Ballybunion. (Courtesy of John deGarmo)

on. Eventually, the match reached the eighteenth green and all the members and visitors present rushed out to see the final outcome. After getting a look at Harnett, the club president at the time, Brendan Kelly, was heard to remark, "I did not know we had a Zulu on our team."

On another occasion, Harnett, who earned his living as a bank official, was selected to represent his organization in a keenly contested interbank match. As luck would have it, Bill was drawn to play against an obviously much inferior opponent, who happened to be a Board Director of the opposing bank. Before setting out to play, Bill was approached by his own team captain and told "to go easy" on his opponent because the poor fellow was only filling in as a last-minute replacement and would be out of his depth. After six holes, the captain met Bill, head down and obviously concentrating hard, striding determinedly toward the seventh tee.

"How are you going, Bill?"

"Six up."

"Didn't I tell you to take it handy?"

"Blank off!"

Going from the ninth green to the tenth tee, the team

captain and player met yet again.

"How's it going now, Bill?"

"Nine up."

"Jaysus, Bill, didn't I ask you to go easy? That man is only making up numbers. And besides, he is a Director!"

"Blank off!"

At the tenth, Bill's opponent made a valiant effort to restore some pride, but his shot kicked unluckily into the cavernous bunker just off the green on the right. As he was going down into the bunker the poor man lost his footing and fell into the sand, grounding his club in the process. Bill rushed forward—not to the man's assistance, but to claim the hole and match! When Bill's teammates heard about this, they were disgusted and shunned him in the clubhouse afterward. He was left to eat and drink alone. After a suitable cooling off period, somebody approached Bill, who, it must be said, was normally a most affable and warm person.

"Why did you do it, Bill? What did that poor man ever do to you?"

"It is like this," replied Bill. "The shagger had a bag of peppermints the whole way round and he never offered me one!"

The late Pat Mulcare, who died at 52 in 1998, was surely the club's greatest ever player. No matter what the circumstances, he always played the game in an exemplary, brisk manner with no affectation whatsoever. He had a distinctive, proud walk due to his training as a policeman, and strode the fairways with a bearing that would make you think he owned them and would brook no nonsense from anyone. Placing the ball well forward in his stance, he grounded the club up to six inches behind the ball. He then moved "into" his shots with supreme grace and timing, confidently attacking every one without a hint of fear.

After winning the annual scratch cup tournament at Ballybunion early in the 1970s, I made a fairly strong speech in the clubhouse in which I gave Mulcare a public tongue-lashing for his cavalier and "could-not-care-less" attitude toward golf. I bemoaned the fact that he could be a world-beater if he tried harder (the irony being that I tried too hard myself). Pat was amused rather than offended, and "for my penance" forced me to drink my first ever pint of Guinness. Subsequently he went on to outperform me by a considerable margin, while never appearing to change his casual approach. He "three-peated" the East of Ireland Championship—which I used to regard as the *real* amateur championship of Ireland because it is a 72-hole stroke-play event—and also "the South" at Lahinch. He made an excellent Walker Cup appearance at St. Andrews in 1975 against a team of American all-stars that included Jerry Pate, George Burns, Craig Stadler, Jay Haas, Curtis Strange, Vinny Giles, and Gary Koch.

Ballybunion Golf Club had a green fee income of well over one million Irish punts ($1.4 million) in 1998. If anybody had forecast that just twenty years earlier, when the annual sub was only IR£42-35p ($60) including GUI Poll Tax, and the daily green fee was IR£3.00 ($5), they would have been considered mad. Today the club is awash with funds, thanks to the unbelievable income generated by overseas visitors. In the past twenty years, a second world-class course (designed by Robert Trent Jones) was added, as well as a IR£3 million-plus clubhouse and a fine practice ground with facilities costing IR£500,000 ($700,000). In 1998 a completely new, fully automatic watering system was installed on both courses at the not inconsiderable cost of IR£750,000 (approximately $1 million). On top of all that, a further IR£3 million ($4.5 million) has been spent on the pivotal coastal erosion project since it began in 1977. All of this expenditure has been paid for principally out of green fee income. (All conversions to dollar equivalents are approximate and I have taken into account the ever changing exchange rates.)

It should never be forgotten that if the "Save Ballybunion Golf Club Fund" undertaken in 1976 as the brainchild of Sean Walsh and Jackie Hourigan had not suc-

ceeded, parts of the course would be under the sea by now
because erosion was so much out of control. More than
coastal erosion was threatening the existence of the place.
There was also a Sword of Damocles being wielded by a
bank manager, under pressure from his head office. It is
impossible to exaggerate how poor the financial state of
the club was at that time and throughout most of its existence. A couple of small events miraculously changed
everything. In 1976, an overdraft of IR£40,000 ($65,000)
was ongoing, without any impression being made on it.
Enough was enough as far as that particular bank manager
was concerned. Club Captain Jackie Hourigan, provoked
by the bank's rejection of a simple application for an extra
loan of £85 ($160) to purchase a new carpet for the club-
house, was stung into radical action and with Sean Walsh
conceived and founded the "Save Ballybunion Golf Course
Fund." Unwittingly, the banker had sparked a series of
unstoppable events, the end result of which is today's millionaire status of the club's finances.

One of the first projects undertaken was to try to entice
new members to join the club. Each member of the nine-
man club management committee undertook to find five
new members. Not one of them succeeded in filling his quota.
There was no entrance fee involved either, just the annual
subscription of £40 ($60) would do. Compare that to today:
Membership is closed, and it could be some years before it
will open again. There are 650 overseas life members who
paid a hefty fee measured in thousands of dollars to join.

You can be sure that when the club does open its doors
to new members once again, an entrance fee of enormous
proportions will be part of the deal. Visitor tee times
between the beginning of March and the end of October
have to be booked months in advance. There is a waiting
list as long as your arm all summer long hoping for cancel-
lations. Anybody who turns up speculatively can only play
if he is lucky enough to find a kind member who will introduce him and play with him during the limited times set

aside for members each day. Until recent years there was an almost fatal shortage of members. In the year 2000 the annual fee was still one of the lowest in the country at IR£200 ($240). My first annual subscription in 1962 was three guineas (that is, three pounds and three shillings, or IR£3.15, or $10).

The real beginning of the change in fortunes can be traced back to 1969, when the famous American golf writer Herbert Warren Wind turned up unannounced and played with the club manager, Sean Walsh. Subsequently Mr. Wind wrote an elegant piece in *The New Yorker* magazine, in which he made an almost throwaway remark that Ballybunion was the finest seaside links he had ever played. Almost immediately a trickle of American visitors began to arrive. The trickle turned into a flood when Tom Watson extolled Ballybunion's virtues to the world's golf media after his 1982 British Open win at Muirfield. Watson had come to County Kerry on the prompting of his friend, USGA President Sandy Tatum, during the week prior to going over to Scotland, so that he could sharpen his seaside golf skills. Such visits by Watson and many other stars of the U.S. PGA Tour have become annual talisman-like rituals ever since. Mark O'Meara was the latest American to achieve success via the Ballybunion route when he won at Royal Birkdale in 1998. Eventually Tom Watson was elected an Honorary Life Member of the club for his contribution to its dramatic development, and he was allowed to make a number of design changes to the course that have been well received. Then his fellow members heaped further honour upon Watson by electing him their Club Captain for the 2000 millennium.

It seems like another lifetime to me now that once upon a time I went to Ballybunion almost every weekend with Father Enright, James Carew, Billy Rice, Vincent Nevin, Garry Geary, the late Sean Moran, and Father Liam Kelly. My friends and I often had the course to ourselves and we had no difficulty playing 36 holes, which we did more often than not. Because clubhouse catering was nonexistent, we brought our own sandwiches, or hot stew in flasks, for "halftime" sustenance. Even the route we used to get to the course has changed completely since the location of the clubhouse was moved and the town itself became clogged with people and traffic.

The golf course was much rougher and more natural looking than it is now. It was also a good deal shorter. Lack of length continues to be Ballybunion's greatest single drawback. The course has always needed wind to help it to protect itself. This was proven beyond all doubt when the "big boys" came to town for the Irish Open in June 2000. While (most uncharacteristically) the wind stayed away, the pros simply killed par. When only the slightest hint of wind and rain had to be contended with on the weekend, the scores went up noticeably.

In the 1960s, the clubhouse was located where the tuck (refreshment) shop beside the sixth tee is now, and would easily have passed for a barn or a machinery shed to the passing onlooker. The changing facilities could be described as primitive at best. The bar was spartan and basic, and it filled to overflowing in no time at all. The present sixth hole was the first, and the current fifth was the eighteenth. Both worked well as opening and finishing holes. I was somewhat amused that for the playing of the Irish Open in 2000, the event reverted to this original and better, in my opinion, sequence of play.

The most vivid memory I have of those days of yore was how savage the rough was. It was never cut and it featured tall, wispy, meadow grasses as well as an amazing variety of orchids and other wild flowers in many and varied colours. The combination of golfer traffic and chemicals has eliminated much of the flora and fauna from the links—the fauna being rabbits that, at one time, almost overran the place, and I am not referring to those of the golfing variety either. Balls often went into burrows and one always had to keep an eye out while searching in the rough in case one

*Spectacular but punishing dunes on both sides of the 16th fairway on
Ballybunion's Old Course mean you will be forced to go mountain climb-
ing after your ball if you do not keep to the straight and narrow. (Michael
Diggin Photography)*

might put one's foot into one and break a leg. In the final of
the Irish Close Championship in 1979, Jackie Harrington's
ball went down a rabbit hole at a vital stage in the match,
but fortunately someone in the crowd saw it and after a lot
of digging it was retrieved and Jackie survived the scare and
won. Today, opportunities for such excitement are few and
far between. The rough, though still tough, is less fierce
than it used to be. This is understandable because of the
number of players trying to get around. Play would simply
slow down to a crawl if members and visitors spent as much
time as we did looking for golf balls. When Father Enright
and I played the course in the 1960s, we rarely took more
than two hours and thirty minutes to complete 18 holes.
Now the average round takes four and a half hours!

Over the years, I have watched with dismay as the tex-
ture of the fairway turf has become muddier, heavier, and
less sandy. There were several cries of "Stop!" by members

at various annual general meetings, but to no avail. Muddy lies were never a factor, even in the height of winter. But now, worm casts are visible all year round, with disastrous consequences for the fairways. I blame overwatering and fertilisers. In summer, the greens used to be glassy and it was almost impossible to stop a ball on them. Now it is no bother to stop the balata ball dead in its tracks with an approach shot. The introduction of new bunkering and the lengthening of some holes have made the course more difficult, but it is still on the short side for top class players on a calm day.

In 1975, the officers of the club went to Dublin to ask the Irish Tourist Board for money to help them with the cost of tackling the serious coastal erosion that was threatening the links. They were laughed at, and told there was no tourist potential in golf. It was a minority, elitist sport, and as there were no votes in it for politicians, they would not fund it. In 1979, another deputation, led by Jackie Hourigan, Sean Walsh, and Flor O'Connor, met the American arm of the same organization in New York. The Tourist Board was still singing the same tune. They said they had spent $100,000 trying to entice American golfers to come to Ireland that year and only fifty had come.

"The weather in Ireland does not suit American golfers," was how the Tourist chiefs saw it, but their research was out of date and already the rush had begun. Within a few years the place was positively flooded with golfers in funny hats and the latest in graphite weaponry. For Americans, golf in Ireland had become costproof, weatherproof, and warproof. As little as ten years earlier, nobody would have forecast that in 1998 there would be 245,000 visiting golfers to Ireland from overseas.

To illustrate how bad the erosion was, I remember witnessing scratch football games taking place to the right of the seventh fairway well out of the way of the passing golfers. The original seventh green, which was a nightmare to reach with a long iron approach, has long since fallen into the sea. There were twenty yards of dry land behind the tenth green, and plenty of ground right of the eleventh fairway and to the right of the seventeenth fairway. It is certain that these irreplaceable holes along the shoreline would have been lost to the sea without the fortifications that were installed.

When Sean Walsh was Club Captain for the centenary year in 1993, he thought he would like to help the club to win the blue riband of Irish golf, the Irish Senior Cup for the club. He gathered together what he himself termed a team of "all-stars." These fellows, myself included, were all members of Ballybunion, but our playing allegiances usually rested elsewhere. When I was invited to join the panel, I accepted in spite of my previous unshakeable loyalty to Limerick. As I was only on the periphery of the Limerick team by then, and ready to be booted out for good, due to "old age" and a fading game, I thought I would be forgiven if I jumped ship on a "once and once only basis." Besides which, Sean Walsh was always so kind to me over the years in his capacity as Club Manager, that I did not want to refuse him. On the morning of our first match, Sean called Pat Mulcare and me aside and told us he could not make up his mind which of us to select for action. He asked us to go out and play the last four holes and report back to him which of us was playing better. We were both completely at odds with our games and we ploughed our way back to the clubhouse. Simultaneously we declared neither of us was fit and somebody else should be asked to play. We were ordered to produce a scorecard. When Sean totalled it up, I had taken one stroke less thanks to a double-bogey five at the fifteenth against Mulcare's six! That decided it. I was forced into action. To my eternal shame, I received the worst walloping of my entire career at the hands of a young and eager Gerard O'Sullivan from Tralee. Pat looked on with some amusement that it was I, and not he, making an "eejit" of himself. In the afternoon match, it was his turn to be humiliated by a much younger and hungrier opponent, and the team of all-stars was soundly beaten.

Sean Walsh's enormous contribution to the club's development and its position in world golf today cannot be underestimated. Without him it would not have happened. There would be no million punts of green fee revenue, no swanky clubhouse, and no Cashen Course. There were others involved, too, but Sean was the main man. The famous English golf correspondent, the late Peter Dobereiner, was a great fan of Ballybunion. He stated in print several times that people like Sean Walsh were national treasures and an endangered species, and that they should be cherished and appreciated for their efforts to please their fellow man. How perfectly appropriate! Sean, without any staff to help him, was the welcoming face who spent long hours of attendance at the club without the benefit of modern inventions like time sheets and faxes. He understood golf and golfers. He knew the enjoyment of the game was paramount and that everything else was secondary. He found a way to get everyone onto the course even when the crowds started to come. He had an incredible memory for names and for people's status in golf. If you visited Ballybunion once, he had your name and your calibre as a golfer forever. Critically, he was universally popular with the gentlemen of the media, which is never a disadvantage when you are trying to promote something. No club anywhere ever had a better promoter than Sean. These days the club is more like a factory. It is efficient but it does not have the heart and warmth that once were there. Sadly, this was inevitable. It is the price you pay for a million-punt empire.

The progress made has not been all beneficial: The members have had to make huge sacrifices by handing over so many of their tee times to visitors. Casual golf is nonexistent except on very rare specific days, which sounds like a contradiction but it is a fact. Club competitions are always oversubscribed and it is difficult to get on the time sheets. It is only when I have overseas visitors bursting to play Ballybunion that I make the extra effort needed to get a game. It's a big change from the days when you could arrive without booking in advance and get off without delay. Until the mid-1980s, when Father Enright ceased playing, I played far more at Ballybunion than I did at Lahinch. But because of the decreasing number of tee times available due to Watson's "guests," I gradually drifted away and became a regular at Lahinch instead.

Still, I am proud of my long association with the club, being a member since 1962. When life memberships were offered to raise much-needed funds for the erosion project, I was one of the first to subscribe. The "Save Ballybunion Fund" was slow getting up a head of steam until Dr. John Leahy and I prompted Limerick Golf Club to organize an open week of golf events to raise funds. The spoils were handed over in a carefully orchestrated blare of publicity. Other clubs up and down the land soon followed our example and the badly needed money began to roll in. Tom Watson took care of the American dimension later with his priceless remarks while holding the old claret jug itself in his arms. That was the clincher.

The biggest flaw at Ballybunion has been evident for years, and many members and visitors alike agree that the eighteenth hole is a huge disappointment and an anticlimax, similar to the situation at Cypress Point in California. When this hole was the thirteenth it did not seem so bad, but as a finishing hole it is awful. Tom Watson designed some worthwhile and laudable improvements to it, but it still requires a more radical rebuild. Turning it into a long par three with the green below the clubhouse is one suggestion, but there are other alternatives, too.

When I think back on what Ballybunion was like in 1962, when I had my first round of golf there with Father Gerry Enright and the "old pro" himself, Brendan Houlihan, I think of the rough and a story about a Limerick man named Tommy O'Donnell, a former President of the Golfing Union of Ireland. O'Donnell was a competitor in the 1958 Irish Close Championship. At the tenth hole, as we know it today, his opponent "let one go on the wind" and after a

The much criticized blind 18th green and clubhouse on Ballybunion's Old Course. (Michael Diggin Photography)

long time looking for the ball in vain, gave up, conceded the hole, and began his march to the next tee. Upon arriving there he noticed Tommy was still searching. He called and waved but the search went on. It emerged that Tommy had put his bag down in the high grass and couldn't find it!

The future looks bright for Ballybunion. One of its biggest problems in the future will be what to do with all of that revenue. I suggest further work on the Cashen Course—especially the footpaths—and possibly a third course. A par-three or nine-hole layout would do, if there is a limit on available land. That would facilitate junior and senior golfers alike. When the new clubhouse was built, it should have contained bedrooms for visiting golfers. Imagine what you could charge for Bed & Breakfast and a game of golf. The extra income thus generated would have allowed the membership to reclaim some of the tee times given up to visitors.

⊛

CHAPTER 9

Ballyclough

A personal perspective on my home club

The late Dr. Michael Cagney was one of the great characters at Limerick Golf Club, affectionately known as Ballyclough by its members. My father thought so highly of Dr. Mick that he invited him to be his vice captain in 1968, and a wise and popular choice it was. Mick was a terrific sportsman, excelling at several disciplines, including winning a rugby blue at University College, Cork. But it utterly perplexed him that he was such a poor golfer.

One day Mick was sitting in the bar after a particularly frustrating round. Depressed and fed up, he wailed out loud to anybody who would listen, "I must easily be the worst golfer playing at Ballyclough."

The late Dr. Noel McMahon rose to the bait and shouted over, "Oh no, you're not. I am!"

Now, Dr. Noel and Dr. Mick were the best of friends, and frequent companions on the golf course. Every now and again, when Billy Rice and I were the two best players in the club, we were roped in to be their partners in an all-out effort to win a turkey or Christmas hamper. Billy and I tried to arrange it so that we would pair with them in Scotch Foursomes format—that is, two drives are played from the tee, the best positioned ball is selected to play out

Giving it a lash from the first tee at Ballyclough during the Roberts Cup of 1968.

the rest of the hole, playing alternately. That way, Rice and I could play most of the golf and make full use of our partner's maximum handicap allowance. On one memorable occasion, Billy was dumbfounded to be requested to play his partner's ball to the final green from about 200 yards. This was in spite of the fact that he himself had launched a magnificent drive to within 75 yards of the putting surface. Undaunted, Billy successfully found the green with a three-iron and Cagney secured the Christmas hamper by holing the vital birdie putt from 25 feet.

After a bit of pantomiming "Oh no, you're not!" and "Oh yes, I am!" between the two friends, they decided that they should play a match to find out, once and for all, who the worst golfer at Ballyclough really was—all in good fun, of course. Michael's depression evaporated the instant the side bets were struck. His normal optimistic outlook returned and he began looking forward to the battle ahead, and planning the downfall of his friend.

I was requisitioned to caddie for him and Billy Rice was purloined to look after Noel. The wager negotiated was fifty quid—almost a month's wages to the less affluent caddies. Going down the third fairway, Mick whispered to me that he could not lose.

"If I win, I will no longer be recognized as the worst player in the club. But if I lose, I will finally be "acclaimed" beyond contradiction. Either way, I cannot lose!" he said.

It took me some time to work out what precisely he was telling me. To make a long story short, the golf played was fairly horrendous but it was nip and tuck all the way. With three holes to go, the match was all square. Billy innocently asked, "What happens if you finish all square, boys?"

The look of consternation on both faces told it all. Neither of them had thought of that! This was war and it would be a fight until death. Both players zigzagged their way down the simple, straightaway drive-and-a-wedge (for me) seventeenth hole. Miraculously, Cagney holed a monster putt from the edge of the green for a winning bogey five. One up, one to go. When they teed up on the eighteenth, a small crowd of curious, morbid vultures spilled out from the Clubhouse and began to place side bets. With his arms leaden and weighed down by tension, Mick skimmed his way up the fairway. Four daisy cutters left him five yards short of the putting surface. Noel, motivated by the sight of the hangman's noose, hit his two best shots of the day to about twenty yards short of the green. Advantage McMahon. Shank. Another shank. Then a desperate and despairing skull followed. Miraculously, the ball struck the flagstick and stopped less than a foot away. Down in six, surely. I told Mick to take out his putter and "whack it." Somehow he managed to get within five feet of the hole on the steeply inclined green. After much sighing and heavy breathing he sank the putt. To this day it remains one of the most courageous putts I ever saw holed. He had won. He was not the worst golfer in the club after all. Victor and

vanquished threw their arms around each other and
marched into the clubhouse to buy drinks all round. Both
accepted the result with grace. It is only now, writing this
down, that I realize Dr. Mick was correct. It did not matter
who won or lost. In fact, does it ever? It has been the proud
tradition for well over a hundred years to produce players
with the spirit of Mick Cagney and Noel McMahon at
Ballyclough. Their attitude and example has been handed
down through the generations. Thankfully, some of the
golfers happened to become good enough to win Irish and
International Championships along the way.

Limerick Golf Club is the third oldest golf club in the
Republic of Ireland, founded in 1891 by Sir Alec Shaw and a
few friends—some of whom were members of the Scottish
Black Watch Regiment, garrisoned in Limerick at the time.
The club had a chequered early history, changing location
several times before it finally settled in its present abode in
1919 as a nine-hole layout. In 1927, Dr. Alister MacKenzie,
the famous British architect, was brought over to redesign
Lahinch. He was inveigled by Shaw to come to Limerick,
and a number of changes were made and new holes were
laid out. It brought the course up to a full eighteen.

Although Limerick Golf Club is one of the earliest
members of the Golfing Union of Ireland, and Alec Shaw
was one of its first vice presidents, the club kept a low pro-
file for the first sixty years or so of its existence. Then in the
1950s, led by Eddie O'Brien and the Daly boys, Eddie and
John, who were sons of Willie Daly, the long-serving club
professional, the club developed some players with above
average ability and an understandable desire to prove it
nationally. There was sporadic success at the Munster level
until 1967, when the Barton Shield was won at Rosses
Point, the club's first All-Ireland title. From then on the
club has been one of the most successful and consistent
winners on the field of play, and it has developed a feared
and admired tradition.

The golf season in Ireland, at all levels of the game,

*Limerick GC (Ballyclough). Winners of the Irish Senior Cup of 1980.
Standing (left to right): Michael Roberts, Jack Lynch, Pat Walsh, Billy
Rice, Michael Galvin, Ivan Morris. Sitting (left to right): Jackie
Harrington, John Holmes (nonplaying captain), Vincent Finucane (club
captain), Tom Morris (club president), Vincent Nevin.*

revolves around team matches for club, county, province,
and country. There are provincial and all-Ireland interclub
competitions for everybody from the humble eighteen
handicapper down to the elite scratch man. There are the
Barton Shield and Irish Senior Cup for the Category 1 players of three handicap and lower; the Irish Junior Cup for
handicaps 4.5 and upward; the James Bruen Shield for 6
handicaps and upward; the Purcell Shield for 12 handicaps
and upward; the Fred Daly Trophy for those under the age
of 17; and the Joe Carr Trophy for the over 60 set.
Everybody is catered to in one way or another. Each competition is played off by team match-play format at
regional, provincial, and all-Ireland levels. For those left
standing, the all-Ireland finals are played each September

amid great tension and excitement and in front of partisan and emotional galleries. Any team that manages to qualify for the finals can be assured of tremendous support from their fellow club members. It can be highly pressurized for the players, but it gives them a real feeling for what it must be like to compete at the highest levels of the game.

In a 1961 heat wave at Lahinch, a team of Patrick J. Walsh, Nick McMahon, Paddy McPolin, Garry Geary, and Kevin Hayes came within a heartbeat of winning the premier title in Irish Club golf, the Irish Senior Cup. However, a Shandon Park team, containing five Internationals, had a tincture too much class for our boys. That near miss set the club, including me, alight with ambition. But it took another six years before a national title was won at last. The team of Billy Rice, Garry Geary, Vincent Nevin, and myself, with Nick McMahon as Team Captain, won the Barton Shield (the Irish Foursomes Team Championship). This group went on to spearhead a golden age of achievement for the club over the next twenty years. I am proud that I was part of all that. I was inspired by those who showed me the art of the possible and helped by the fact that, unlike the young golfers of today, I had a free run on the course and was allowed to play and practice as much as I liked.

There was a lovely putting and bowling green in front of the old wooden clubhouse at Limerick, where I spent many hours. I have fond memories of my brother Dermot—as a small boy still in short pants—hustling six-penny bets with anybody who dared to set foot on it. The practice ground was almost my personal property, as Aidan Larkin, Geoff Keogh, and myself were possibly the only persons who used it regularly. There was no such thing as junior golf, which was just as well because the standard of coaching was dire. Instead, I learned the game through observation and reading magazines. Much of the stuff I read or was told was damaging and misleading. Club professional Willie Daly was a master clubmaker and superb greenskeeper, but he was a hopeless teacher. The youngsters nowadays are far better coached, but they need to be given more time and space to play to be able to take advantage of it. I had no restrictions put in my way and most of the time had my own private golf course to play on. This allowed me to learn the game in blissful comfort. It was no problem for me to play two or even three rounds in a day. One day I managed 85 holes, having cycled seven miles in the predawn darkness all the way across town with my bag of clubs on my back. Sunday afternoons were particularly quiet. I used to meet Father Enright at 1:00 P.M., and we would gallop off to play 36 holes without a break or the slightest interference from anybody. There were not enough players to warrant a time sheet. About three or four fourballs of lady golfers played on Sunday afternoons. We had it judged to perfection. We nearly always had a clear run on the course and it took us only two hours and twenty minutes to play 18 holes.

One Sunday we were having a great set-to when I suddenly caught fire on the back nine and made five birdies on the trot. Coming off the sixteenth green, I realized it was getting late. As I had not been to Mass, I told my reverend friend that I had better stop playing and leave. He was aghast.

"You cannot go now. You only need one birdie for a 29. I will give you a dispensation. Go to mass tomorrow instead. Play on!" he ordered.

I need hardly tell you there was no way the gods of golf would tolerate such cavalier behaviour toward worship. Not only did I not do my 29 then, but I have not managed to do so since.

Ballyclough may not appear to be the most difficult course in the world, but low scores have been very scarce on it—even top class tournament professionals have found it unyielding. Why this should be so is difficult to pinpoint. The flatness of the approaches to most of the greens hampers accurate judgment of distance, while anyone missing a green is faced with a tricky pitch over the many endearing humps and bumps that are the trademark of all MacKenzie courses.

The main barrier to low scoring at my home course, as I see it, is the relatively poor soil and quality of grass on the fairways, which makes iron play to unreceptive greens unpredictable. Over the past twenty years, the wide open nature of the course has gradually disappeared, thanks to several vigorous tree planting programs. No less an authority than Dr. MacKenzie agrees with me that the tree planters have gone too far. The good Doctor himself wrote that "narrow fairways, bordered by trees or long grass makes for bad golfers, destroying the harmony and continuity of the game, and causing a cramped style of play." Fairway targets are too tight, and the dogleg shapes of tree-lined fairways result in an unacceptable number of blind approach shots from the centre of the fairway. In fast-running conditions, all of those trees—which have grown out as well as up— drive me mad. I passionately believe planting trees too close to the path of play is a mistake, and I was glad to read in Dr. MacKenzie's book, *The Spirit of St. Andrews*, that the greatest golf course architect of them all felt the same way. Trees damage soil and grass growth, block out the sun, prevent the air from circulating, and send their underground roots all over the place, damaging drains and undermining green foundations. Worst of all, they interfere with golf's greatest pleasure: hitting the ball. There are few things more annoying than having to chip sideways or play backwards because a tree is in the way. A tree should be an obstacle that you can play around, over, or under, but it should *never* be an obstruction. Trees are needed sometimes to frame or shape a hole. In that case, trees with five feet of air beneath the branches are the only situation that is acceptable to me.

"Playing down fairways bordered by straight lines of trees is not only inartistic, but it makes for tedious and uninteresting golf.... [Courses are] ruined by planting rows of trees like soldiers along the borders of fairways.... [However] groups of trees, planted irregularly, can create fascinating golf.... Some of the most spectacular shots I have seen have been around, over or through narrow gaps in trees...."

Those words were written by Dr. MacKenzie. I have been saying the same thing to Committee members for twenty years, only to be ignored as if I were a crank. Now there is no need for me to say another word about the matter!

When Ballyclough was relatively wide open, it cultivated better players, who had no fear or inhibitions. Nor was the game really any easier. The hole was still four and a quarter inches in diameter, and greens still had to be approached from the correct spot on the fairway to achieve maximum results. An extra inch of grass growth in the rough is a fairer hazard or obstacle to be overcome. My idea of a perfect use of mature trees is at the great Robert Trent Jones Sr's Adare Golf Club. My fellow members do not have to travel very far to see what I mean.

The best hole at Ballyclough is the 384-yard dogleg-right fourth. You must drive over a gentle crest, and at its apex the fairway turns to the right but slopes to the left. This presents a few problems, with trees acting like magnets on both sides. A left-to-right-shaped drive must pitch on a fairly small area on the fairway to stay on. Four bunkers in front and trees at the back beautifully frame the slightly elevated green. There is a severe fall-off on the left, and the green slopes sharply from back right to front left. It's an altogether excellent hole. If it were fifty yards longer, it would be world class.

The par-five sixth is a new hole, having been created during the mid-1980s by Michael Galvin, Eamonn McInerney, and yours truly. It is a genuine par five, rarely reachable in two, and only then by taking a huge risk with the tee shot. It is a good hole that calls for a bit of thought as well as straight, controlled hitting. It would be even better if the teeing ground were positioned further to the left, as was originally planned. A stream on the left is a constant hazard, as it diagonally crosses the fairway twice before finally getting out of the way close to the green. The stream's meandering presence is well capable of undermining a nervous player. The design team had planned that the stream would pass even closer to the green than it does now, but we were thwarted.

The seventh is a Firestone Country Club–type hole. It's long, straight, and tree-lined, but because the fairway is reasonably wide the hole is fair and a fine challenge. On the back nine, holes ten and twelve are key. Both are longish, dogleg par fours infested by trees. After negotiating them successfully, the only potential disaster remaining is the short fourteenth, which has Dr. John Leahy's garden lurking to claim the slightest tweak to the left. The good Doctor could make a small fortune recycling golf balls that enter his property, but he has an admirable tolerance and forbearance toward his fellow golfers.

There was a time when big hitters like Billy Rice, Kevin Hayes, and Tim Duggan drove straight onto the fifteenth and sixteenth greens, but this is not possible anymore, due to the tees being put back and the maturing trees forcing new lines of attack. Even Tiger could not take these greens on when he played the course in 2000.

Before Limerick Golf Club developed its successful teams and players of the 1960s and later, there were a few excellent players produced by the club who should not be forgotten. Stanley Martyn was a first class player in the 1920s and 1930s. A small, bespectacled, studious looking man, he could hit the ball a mile with a most unusual collection of clubs. He only had eight clubs in his arsenal, including two three-irons and two seven-irons. He distinguished them as "heavy" and "light," and each had an entirely different capability. Stanley came close to winning the South of Ireland Championship at Lahinch a number of times, being beaten in successive finals in 1932 and 1933. It was the John Burke era, but Stanley lost both finals to another of the all-time great players of Irish amateur golf, Joe Brown from Tramore. Frank Hannon, who was a frequent user of the practice ground at Ballyclough until a ripe old age (whistling while he swung), lost the 1941 "South" final to the practically unbeatable Burke. Gerry Gilligan won the "South" in 1951. It was one of the biggest surprises of all time, because he was no better than a four handicapper and never contended before or since.

On the 9th of September, 1937, the club hosted an extraordinary exhibition match between eleven-time major champion Walter Hagen and the famous trick shot artist, Joe Kirkwood, and Limerick club members Stanley Martyn and John Burke. John was a resident of Limerick City, but he was more usually associated with Lahinch. Although there was massive publicity in advance of the match, for some strange reason no reports of the game appeared in the newspapers afterward. The late former club president, Dr. Michael Roberts, was the referee and scorekeeper on that day, and he told me it was a great occasion and the homesters actually won by two holes. A giant marquee was erected and a massive crowd attended. The Americans were particularly impressed by Burke, and Hagen prevailed on John to give him a lesson on the running four-iron chip, up and over the bank on the left of the fourth green (then the fifteenth and close to the clubhouse), after the match. Kirkwood had a rubber-shafted rogue driver. He invited all comers to give it a try. Burke took up the challenge and hit a beauty. Kirkwood said it was the first time that any player had managed to *hit* the ball, let alone perfectly.

There has been a great golfing tradition at Ballyclough for much of its long history. The social side of golf has always been second to the playing of the game. It is a pity that the club was not more avaricious for land some years ago because it could badly do with another 18 holes to cater to everybody who wants to play now. For many years the survival of the club was so shaky, I suppose it was inevitable that there would be a certain lack of courage, foresight, and ambition. It is sad to relate that I can remember several crucial Annual General Meeting where the members rejected opportunities to purchase land that would have eased the overcrowding problems we suffer today. This was unlike the attitude of Sir Alec Shaw and Company at the beginning, who, within one year of starting their golf course in Limerick, were actively searching further afield for a summer retreat on links territory. They took little time to find the "perfect ground" at Lahinch, which was founded and opened by a group comprised entirely of Limerick Golf Club members in 1892, only one year after the Limerick Club itself was up and running.

❁

Chapter 10

Ballybunion versus Lahinch

A surprising result

I have been a member of Ballybunion G.C. since 1962 and Lahinch G.C. since 1967. Frequently I am asked to compare them. Without thinking too deeply, the vast majority of golfers will tell you straight up that Ballybunion is at least a couple of shots harder than Lahinch. But does this stand up to closer scrutiny?

Back when I was a fairly decent player, I invariably returned lower scores at Ballybunion than I ever did at Lahinch. The lower par rating of 71 as against 72 partially accounted for this, but the relative shortness of the Ballybunion links and the fact that Lahinch can be stretched to up to 300 yards longer is significant.

Because Ballybunion rewards good shots more consistently, and punishes off-line shots more severely, its good score/bad score spread is noticeably wider than it is at Lahinch. It is considerably easier to scramble your way around Lahinch when "off your game." Ballybunion is recognized as a fantastic second shot course. Most of the greens are slender and elevated, which is a double-edged sword. The target may be more elusive, but shots on target are rewarded by realistic birdie opportunities. Lahinch, on the other hand, has more challenging tee shots, more blind

Another typical Ballybunion scene. Threading your ball through all those high dunes on a windy day calls for both skill and nerve. (Courtesy of D.K. Davis)

From atop a dune, a wild goat, as befits the Lahinch Golf Club mascot and emblem, keeps a keen eye on the weather and other golfing matters. (Michael Diggin Photography)

shots, and more places where you are at the mercy of an unpredictable bounce. For the average player "strategic" Lahinch is more manageable and enjoyable than "penal" Ballybunion. But that is not the whole story. A proper comparison calls for a full hole-by-hole analysis.

To illustrate how problematical Lahinch can be even for experienced locals, I would like to tell you a story. Some years ago, when my brother Dermot was still single, he entered our Spring Match-Play Tournament, which is more or less the unofficial club championship. He was drawn to play against one of the local tigers, Michael Walsh. Michael is the genial and popular Lahinch Club Steward. He knows every blade of grass on the links on a first name basis. Earlier, Dermot had arranged a very-much-looked-forward-to "après le match" date with a beautiful member of the fairer sex. Going up the fifth hole, it was becoming obvious that a slow-moving group of visitors ahead of them was going to delay matters intolerably. In order to leapfrog the obstruction, Dermot inquired from his equally impatient opponent would he be willing to pick up and move forward to the seventh hole? Michael was all for it. The match turned into a real ding-dong affair, with no quarter given or taken, but then the boys ran into more interference further out the course. Approaching the fourteenth green, Dermot was one up and becoming increasingly anxious about being able to make that date on time.

"Michael, are you a man?" asked Dermot.

"I am," replied Michael. "At least I think I am."

"Why don't we call it all flat, skip fifteen, sixteen, and seventeen, and go up eighteen all square?"

"Right, you're on!" says Michael.

The eighteenth was halved in par fives. But because of the time gained and the fact that the first and second holes were close to the clubhouse, Dermot—who likes to win at golf as much as any man—decided he would see if matters could be resolved by the twentieth green, which is situated right beside the car park. If the match were not over by

then he would forfeit it. Two perfect drives were dispatched up the first (nineteenth) fairway. Both balls were
within a couple of feet of each other. Michael was first to
play his second shot and he hit a cracker.

"Great shot, Michael. That is very close!"

Then Dermot played.

"Great shot, Dermot. That is even closer!"

"Oh no, it is not. You are well inside me."

"Not at all. You are closer."

"No, I am not."

"Yes, you are! Don't I know every inch of this course?"
They nearly came to blows arguing about it.

"Michael, I am so certain that you are the one nearest to
the hole that I dare you to swap balls here and now. I will
putt yours and you putt mine when we get up to the green."

"Okay, all right. You're on! But only because I know you
are closer anyway."

When they walked up the hill to the green, they found that
one ball was four feet away and the other twelve feet away.
Michael's was closer, but he had agreed to putt Dermot's ball.
He missed. Dermot duly popped Michael's ball into the
hole, shook hands, thanked him for the game, and said he
had to run. That would have been the end of the matter if
they had kept quiet about the arrangement. But of course,
both Michael and Dermot had to tell everybody and anybody about the unusual end to their match. When the club
committee heard about it, they felt they could not condone
such a cavalier attitude toward a "major" club competition
and they disqualified both of them. The point of the story is,
you never really know where your ball will finish up at Lahinch.

1. Lahinch: 385 yards, Par 4. Ballybunion: 392 yards, Par 4.
The first tee atmosphere at Lahinch is fabulous and the
opening shot is always an uncompromising challenge. The
uphill second shot requires the sort of strong, accurate play
that ironically one would normally associate with
Ballybunion rather than Lahinch. Miss this green on any

side—long, short, right, or left—at your peril. On Ballybunion's first hole the graveyard and out of bounds fence rarely come into play. Once they are avoided, it is a straightforward hole that is quite easy to birdie. On the other hand, birdies at Lahinch's first are extremely rare. Lahinch one up.

2. Lahinch: 512 yards, Par 5. Ballybunion: 445 yards, Par 4.
The Khyber Pass second hole at Ballybunion is about as tough a par four as you will ever encounter; the second shot is a ten on the Richter Scale. To make it somewhat manageable you need to drive as far as possible so that you can put the most lofted club feasible in your hands. But because the fairway narrows dramatically, this prerequisite is laden with difficulties. The extreme elevation of the green site has no welcome for a fairway metal or long iron approach. Recovering from anywhere around this green is a nightmare. The second hole at Lahinch simply does not compare. It is an easy downhill par five that needs a strong wind in your face to make it a worthwhile challenge. The proposed new version of this hole will be a whole new ball game when it is built, but it will never rival its Kerry sister. Match all square.

3. Lahinch: 151 yards, Par 3. Ballybunion: 220 yards, Par 3.
Difficult decision. Two excellent one-shot holes. Each acts as a good barometer of how you are likely to perform subsequently in the round. If there is a crosswind, it takes a particularly well-struck shot to find either "dance floor." Ballybunion may be the longer hole, but the Lahinch green is smaller and rejects shots more mercilessly. Unusually for Ballybunion, the third green has a large flat apron that has a tendency to gather the ball. The out-of-bounds on the left and greater length clinches the result in Ballybunion's favour. Ballybunion, one up.

4. Lahinch: 428 yards, Par 4. Ballybunion: 498 yards, Par 5.
Lahinch's fourth hole is one of its finest, requiring a bold drive to carry a big hill and then a strong second shot over

a lot of rubbish. Two deep bunkers guard the entrance to a shallow, raised green, and if you go over the back, a dropped shot is a certainty. The fourth at Ballybunion is a short and relatively easy par five. Tom Watson has recently inserted bunkers to catch crooked second shots, narrowing the layup area considerably. But it is still an eminently birdieable hole. Some years ago, I was playing with fellow member Jack Lynch. He pushed his drive and was partially stymied by the house that encroaches in a most obtrusive manner onto the right-hand edge of the fairway about 220 yards from the green. As Jack shaped up to his second shot, the back door burst open and the owner, a feisty lady named Wanda Wilson, rushed out with her hand up like a policewoman and said, "How dare you aim your ball at my house! Please desist at once. I am tired of being forced to replace slates damaged by you wild golfers." Jack was startled by this unexpected intrusion into his concentration, but regaining his composure he assured Mrs. Wilson that her house was in no danger whatsoever. "What is your handicap?" "One, madam," said Jack. "I beg your pardon, sir. Carry on!" Wanda stood back to admire Jack's soaring recovery, which easily cleared the house on its way toward the green. Lahinch wins the hole. Match all square again.

5. Lahinch: 482 yards, Par 5. Ballybunion: 508 yards, Par 5.
Two interesting par fives. Both are deceptively difficult and trouble-laden holes if played carelessly. The blind second shot over Klondyke Hill at Lahinch can be problematic, especially for first-time visitors. Beyond it waits a fabulous undulating green that calls for imaginative and deft pitching and putting. Ballybunion's No. 5 is strewn with nasty bunkers, heavy rough, and an out-of-bounds road that runs all the way along the right-hand side. It is also a much longer hole. Ballybunion one up.

6. Lahinch: 155 yards, Par 3. Ballybunion: 364 yards, Par 4.
Here are two unique holes that are throwbacks to the days

The green at the infamous blind "Dell" hole (the 6th) at Lahinch. From the tee, the shallow green is entirely blind from view, sandwiched as it is between two high dunes. This is the side-on view from the 7th tee. (Michael Diggin Photography)

of natural design. The characteristics of the raw earth were respected and utilized. At Ballybunion, the second shot to a long, slender, plateau green is classic. It needs to be accurate enough to be able to "thread the eye of a needle." The green does not have a single bunker to protect it, but the roller-coaster pitch of the land is bamboozling. The quirky but historical Dell Hole at Lahinch has very little to recommend it in twenty-first century golf. It is time it was put in a glass case like the museum piece that it is. Unfortunately, many of my fellow members do not agree and might want to have me hanged for treason for saying so. Ballybunion wins the hole and goes two up.

7. Lahinch: 399 yards, Par 4. Ballybunion: 423 yards, Par 4.
At Ballybunion, if one is playing to the green on the right it is a tight contest, but if the green on the left is in play,

Lahinch is clearly a far better hole. The tough tee shot at Lahinch—normally straight into the prevailing wind—shades it either way, in my humble opinion. Here is the perfect example of why I believe the tee shots at Lahinch are the more demanding. There is unlimited potential to develop the seventh at Lahinch into one of the best holes in golf. It is a gorgeous sight walking down that fairway toward the ocean. The redesigned "outer" green at Ballybunion is too rarely used. Tom Watson has made a reasonable attempt to recreate the original green, which he could not have actually played onto or seen. The old green suffered badly from erosion and was on the point of falling into the sea when it was dug up and moved inland. That "lost" green was a tantalising target. Like the moving statues we hear about from time to time, I am certain the old seventh green at Ballybunion "moved" when my ball was in the air and approaching it on a few occasions. Lahinch wins the hole. Ballybunion one up.

8. Lahinch: 350 yards, Par 4. Ballybunion: 153 yards, Par 3. Two entirely different types of hole. The blindness of the eighth at Lahinch makes it deceptive even if you play it regularly. It is one of the most difficult tee shots on the course. Leave the fairway on either side at your peril. The proposed new version of this hole retains the same tee box but the green will be moved toward the sea and will overlook the beach. This will make it a bit like the fifth at Royal Portrush. It looks a pretty scary target to me already. The prevailing wind causes the par-three eighth at Ballybunion to play very short. The green gathers the ball from all sides. I made a disgusting hole-in-one at this hole a long time ago. A horrible, ribbed, off-line shot was deflected by the mounds onto the gathering green and was sent careering into the hole. When this was the third hole, I saw another unusual ace here. Playing in the annual scratch cup, a visitor from England named Healy was the culprit. Mr. Healy began his round 3,3,1 (birdie, birdie, eagle). Billy Rice and I were stunned by his immediate retirement and the immortal words, "I can-

The glories of Lahinch. This is the 8th hole—which, unfortunately, is about to disappear.

not do any better than that. I need a gin and tonic." He promptly retired to the clubhouse bar nearby and waited for us to join him after completing the round. By then he was in full flight and was buying drinks for all and sundry. Lahinch wins the hole and the match is all square again.

9. Lahinch: 384 yards, Par 4. Ballybunion: 454 yards, Par 4. The ninth green at Lahinch is one of the original Tom Morris greens, and it can present a number of intriguing problems, requiring great skill and creativity. But the hole in general cannot stand up to Ballybunion's ninth, where a strong drive into position on the left half of the fairway can still leave one with possibly the most difficult second shot on the course. A radar-like medium or long iron to an exposed, elevated green is required to avoid receiving some rather harsh treatment from the large mound on the front right-hand corner of the green. Chipping from either side of this green is next to impossible. I often lay up here and take my chances from in front of the green. A clear win for Ballybunion. Ballybunion turns one up.

The author on the 9th tee at Lahinch.

This is the magnificent view from the 9th tee at Lahinch, the highest point on the course, looking northeast across the 10th, 12th, and 13th holes. (Michael Diggin Photography)

10. Lahinch: 451 yards, Par 4. Ballybunion: 359 yards, Par 4.
Unless you are playing straight into a strong westerly, the
drive at Ballybunion is not too demanding and the second
shot is a relatively easy short iron to a (too) large green. At
Lahinch, a drive over some awful territory to a half-hidden
fairway is followed by a partially blind second shot, often
with a fairway metal. The shot is not made any easier by
having to carry onto an altar-like green well above head
height. A four at Lahinch's tenth is a surrogate birdie. When
the new dogleg hole into the dunes on the left is built, it will
be even more demanding. Lahinch (fighting hard) squares
the match once more.

11. Lahinch: 138 yards, Par 3. Ballybunion: 449 yards, Par 4.
The current eleventh at Lahinch is a very pretty, unique par
three with an original Tom Morris green still extant. It was
laid out during the great man's visit in 1904. It and the
ninth green are all that remain of Old Tom's work. By all
accounts Old Tom enjoyed the hospitality at Lahinch, and
was on site for several months. Furthermore, he had his
daughter to keep him company when taking occasional for-
ays to Limerick to lay out a course for Sir Alec Shaw that
has since been "lost." The present eleventh at Lahinch is
perhaps the easiest hole on the course to birdie. Shoot at
the mound at the back of the green; the ball will invariably
come back down to the hole. The new eleventh being created by Hawtree, however, will be a completely different
"kettle of fish." There won't be any convenient cushions,
and into the wind a rifle will be needed to successfully reach
what looks like a narrow, elusive target. Nothing can compare with Ballybunion's eleventh, though. God made this
one! When Jack Nicklaus came to play the course in 1990,
he did not bother to putt on the tenth green. Instead, he went
straight over to the next tee and stood there with hands on
hips, gazing down the fairway for several minutes. The
beach and ocean are close by on the right and there are for-
bidding dunes over on the left. Nicklaus was heard to say,

This is the 11th green at Lahinch. Along with the 9th, it is one of only two greens that remain unaltered since being built by Old Tom Morris of St. Andrew's fame in 1904. (Michael Diggin Photography)

Very few golfing scenes are more memorable than this one: the 10th green and 11th fairway at Ballybunion Old. It rendered Jack Nicklaus almost speechless. Eventually he came out with, "So this is what [Tom] Watson is always talking about." (Michael Diggin Photography)

John deGarmo, author of The Road to Ballybunion, approaches the 11th green at Ballybunion.

"So this is what Watson is always talking about." Surprise, surprise! Ballybunion wins the hole. Ballybunion one up.

12. Lahinch: 475 yards, Par 4. Ballybunion: 192 yards, Par 3. Two difficult holes. On the surface you would imagine that Lahinch is tougher because you need at least two good shots to reach the green, whereas one good one will do at Ballybee. The much loved, long serving Secretary at Lahinch, the late Brud Slattery, once gave me his thoughts on how the twelfth hole there could be turned into an even better hole. "Flatten the fairway undulations by moving the earth to the left. Create substantial mounds all along the left-hand side, and decorate them with marram grass. This would protect the fairway from flying sand off the beach in stormy weather. Move the green forward and to the right in order to bring the big hollow behind the former, abandoned twelfth green into play." What a hole that would be! However, Martin Hawtree has come up with a different plan. He will lengthen the hole to par-five status by stretching the tee and green further away from each other. I have slight doubts about this myself and think Brud's plan is better. Hopefully, my misgivings will be unfounded. The short twelfth at Ballybunion is very dramatic. But it is not quite as difficult as it looks. The big hill on the left can be used as a cushion to cannon the ball back onto the green, which is bowl-like and no less than forty-five yards deep. A fairly "ordinary" shot played onto the edges of the green is always deflected inward, sometimes setting up a flattering birdie opportunity in the process. After some agonizing, the hole is declared halved. Ballybunion still one up.

13. Lahinch: 273 yards, Par 4. Ballybunion: 484 yards, Par 5.
Two definite birdie holes. The thirteenth at Lahinch is a great short par four. With today's equipment it is possible to drive onto the green with only the slightest assistance from the wind. And yet it is never an easy birdie. If you play for a par you will get it. But if you push too hard for a birdie, you might end up with a bogey or worse. Getting up and down from just short of the green looks "routine," but it is far from it. The thirteenth at Ballybunion is a very short par five. The stream does not come into play very often, and the worst trouble at this hole arises if you go through the green with an overzealous approach. If allowed, I would reduce the length of this hole slightly and make it a tough par four. It's close, but I have to give this one to Ballybunion. Ballybunion two up.

14. Lahinch: 488 yards, Par 5. Ballybunion: 131 yards, Par 3.
Ballybunion's No. 14 is a classic. A typical, long, narrow

green can be very elusive and hard to find. Clubbing is not made any easier because the green is above the player's eye level. Father Enright had a firm rule for playing this hole: Never go through the green. No. 14 at Lahinch is an excellent par four-and-a-half—its best feature being an original, roller-coaster, MacKenzie green that sits beyond a pair of Dolly Parton dunes. Lahinch shades it on account of that wonderful green and approach. Ballybunion one up.

15. Lahinch: 462 yards, Par 4. Ballybunion: 216 yards, Par 3.
The fifteenth at Lahinch has always been an extremely tough par four. Usually played into the prevailing wind, it vies with the ninth at Ballybunion to be regarded as the "the toughest" hole in North Munster. Very few holes are as spectacular looking as Ballybunion's picturesque fifteenth. It calls for a strong, straight-as-a-die long iron or metal wood. The gorgeous two-tiered green seems to edge closer to the Atlantic Ocean each year. Unlike the previous comparison, beauty does not beat brawn. Two great shots are needed to secure par at Lahinch; one will do at Ballybunion. I have to give this one to Lahinch. Match all flat.

16. Lahinch: 195 yards, Par 3. Ballybunion: 490 yards, Par 5.
Leave the straight and narrow at Ballybunion's No. 16 and you will get yourself into serious trouble. Nor does a drive onto the centre of the fairway guarantee a safe haven. You could still be faced with a blind shot from a severe side-hill slope over a big hill. Trouble abounds on both sides all the way from tee to green. Players would be wise to have the latest titanium, cling-on mountaineering equipment with them if the second shot is sprayed right or left—the dunes are that vertical. For all that, eagles are regularly achieved here because it is such a short and reachable par five. The pretty sixteenth at Lahinch is an exciting shot. From the high tee you can see it all happening before you, as I did one sunny evening when I had the most enjoyable of my four (to date) holes-in-one. It could so easily have been disas-

The 16th green on Ballybunion Old is an anachronistic "fly-over." The demanding drive from the 1st tee is aimed directly over this green. More balls land in the famous graveyard in the background than on the 16th green, however, thus interfering with the eternal peace of those at rest therein. The great Jack Nicklaus will not thank me for being reminded that he paid an unplanned visit to the graveyard with his first ever golf shot in County Kerry! (Michael Diggin Photography)

trous because I was playing on my own. Fortunately, an elite gallery of two made the feat honest. The late Willie McCavery and his dog were looking on. Willie was the newly appointed professional at Lahinch in 1927 when MacKenzie arrived to design the course that we play today. He remained as Head Professional for fifty years, and is the father of the incumbent professional at the club, Robert. As was his father, Robert is a master wooden clubmaker. There was a time when a McCavery persimmon driver was a very much sought after piece of equipment. Unfortunately, not anymore. But Bob still handcrafts a limited number of gorgeous wooden

putters. Intended for display purposes only, they can effectively do the job of depositing balls into holes as well as any
of the weird contraptions one sees in use these days. McCavery
Senior was mooching around behind the sixteenth tee half-
looking for golf balls when I arrived to play my tee shot.
When he continued to move around, a bit too close for my
comfort, I glared at him in my best Colin Montgomerie
fashion. My eyes ordered him to be still while I addressed
my shot. A well-struck six-iron shot was dispatched on its
way. It bounced twice and rolled right into the cup. The
silence was deafening. "Did you see that?" says I. "Aye" says
Willie. Not another word was spoken. Obviously, Mr.
McCavery was not too easily impressed. Ballybunion wins
the hole and goes one up with two to play.

17. Lahinch: 437 yards, Par 4. Ballybunion: 385 yards, Par 4.
Ballybunion's spectacular seventeenth may yield more
"oohs and aahs" than its counterpart at Lahinch, but as a
golfing challenge there is no contest between these two.
Lahinch is a considerably longer and much more dangerous
hole. I am delighted to say my long-held wish for this hole
has recently come true. The hills that had to be carried to
reach the formerly blind fairway have been lowered.
Players can at last see all of the hole stretching ahead of
them, plus the eighteenth hole further on, the clubhouse,
and the village beyond. It is all most pleasing, as well as a lot
safer for anybody passing by on the left on the Liscannor
Road. The second shot plays longer than its yardage; two
small sentinel dunes have to be carried, which calls for a
higher approach shot than normal. The ball must land deep
into a "turbulent" green. Two down and two to play at
Lahinch is never "dead." Two fours can get you out of jail,
and that is without your opponent doing much wrong,
either. In a similar position at Ballybunion, two fours would
not be worth "a hat of crabs." Ballybunion's No. 17 is a fabulous visual experience. It features an exciting tee shot
from the highest point on the course (close to heaven, as

One of the most memorable shots in Irish golf is from the elevated 17th tee at Ballybunion Old. The fairway far below turns sharply left and it is possible to overshoot and land on the beach if there is only the slightest bit of wind assistance. (Michael Diggin Photography)

they say). But the relatively easy short iron second to a generous, flat green does not approach the difficulty of the second shot and putting required at Lahinch. Lahinch wins the hole. Match all square and one to go.

18. Lahinch: 533 yards, Par 5. Ballybunion: 379 yards, Par 4. A great finishing hole versus an exceedingly poor one. The finish at Lahinch, in my opinion, is perfect. As a par five, it is a birdie opportunity. But you have to play it well to get it. Any slipups and an ugly six looms. Both the setting and challenge are superb, and one has that nice feeling of "coming home." Despite the excellent changes Tom Watson has made to Ballybunion's home hole, it remains pretty awful.

Elsewhere in the sequence it would be a tolerable hole, but not as a finisher. There is a feeling of going underground that I never enjoy. The green is too hidden away, and the sidewalls can flatter an off-line or skulled shot. Lahinch wins the hole and the match by one up. This is bound to surprise a lot of people and get me into trouble. I will now make matters worse by saying that I believe the extraordinary low scores recorded by the professionals who played in the 2000 Irish Open at Ballybunion would not have been matched at Lahinch. Case closed, as far as I am concerned. And, of course, until the Irish Open comes to Lahinch, I cannot be proven wrong.

In August 1999 the members of Lahinch Golf Club agreed to adopt a brave and ambitious plan that is now well underway. Martin Hawtree, the architect who is also responsible for the successful restoration of Royal Birkdale in England, was engaged and "instructed" to bring back the original spirit of Alister Mackenzie which had been lost and destroyed by the mistaken actions of various club members over the years. Incidentally, one of the guilty ones was my own guru and friend John Burke, who really should have known better. Clearly, John did not realise that a Mackenzie design was timeless and unsurpassable.

The main changes proposed are; the second is going to be lengthened, the hole will be a subtle double dogleg featuring additional fairway traps and a roller coaster green surface. To create space for the new green the third hole will be abandoned. The fourth becoming the new third, it will also be lengthened slightly and the large hill that dominates the tee-shot will be lowered to accommodate the big hit that will be needed to reach the fairway. The fifth and sixth are to remain unscathed except for their numeric sequence. There is to be a new green site closer to the beach at the sixth (old seventh). The new seventh will be a short, but rather terrifying, dogleg to the left. The tee-shot is identical to the one employed when playing the old eighth but the new green will sit on a dune over-looking the

beach to such an extent that it will create the most intimidating approach shot, especially on a windy day. I see this as
potentially the most controversial and least popular of all
of the changes. But we will have to wait and see, won't we?

The new eighth will be a short hole of 170 yards, played
with the player's back to the sea, up to a green exquisitely
positioned in a saddle underneath the ninth tee. The ninth
hole will also to be lengthened. By lowering some dunes, a
better view of the landing area on the fairway will be created. The large trap to the right of the green is to be moved
directly into the line of approach and the hillock beside the
green lowered slightly to reduce the number of lucky rico-
chets. The punishing fall off on the left will remain.

Hawtree's back nine is going to be one of the toughest
stretches in all of golf. It will be savagely more difficult than
the old routing. Birdies will be at a premium. The new
tenth will have the same tee shot as before but then the
fairway will turn left into the dunes; the new green will be
sharply raised, just like its predecessor was, and situated in
a classic mini-amphitheatre of dunes. The new par 3
eleventh could be a beast, it will be played out towards the
sea into the prevailing wind and will be considerably longer
than the old order. The current par four twelfth, along the
estuary shore, is to be lengthened to par five status. By
moving the tenth green Hawtree has created the space and
opportunity to weave more magic at the double-green site
formerly shared by Nos.10 and 13. The fourteenth and fifteenth holes, which share a fairway at present, are to be
split. At No. 14, a new tee box, fairway and reduced yardage
will turn it into a demanding par four. No. 15 will retain its
length but the fairway will be narrower. The green will be
elevated and surrounded by deep troughs and traps. I have
always taken 14 and 15 together and put a par nine rating on
them. My approach is unlikely to change even though the
card will tell me otherwise.

The sixteenth and seventeenth greens have also been
raised, reshaped, undulated and re-trapped. Finding the

"dance floor" and recovery, if the target is missed, will be about half a shot harder in each case. All of these alterations will considerably improve the links and cause it to go shooting up the world rankings. The result of my "head-to-head" with Ballybunion will be much easier to defend and no longer scoffed at!

⊛

CHAPTER 11

Doonbeg—Greg Norman's Irish Project

"The sensitivity of this piece of property required a totally hands-on approach," Greg Norman said. "You do not get too many opportunities to work on a piece of land like this one. It is unique. I am going to make sure that the end result is 100 percent. I know that I am not going to please everybody but I will know that I have given it my best effort. This is a course that I want to be identified with. One that I will be able to say with pride, 'I did this one.' I may be the luckiest designer in the world because of the uniqueness of this site. It's Ireland, it's Irish golf, it's links golf; sand dunes like you'll never see again. They're preciously finite."

The enthusiasm of Gregory John Norman is admirable and infectious. Upon meeting him in October of 2000, it was no trouble at all to get him talking about his latest favorite project: the development of a brand new world class golf facility in the middle of nowhere on the extreme west coast of Ireland.

"I love links golf," Norman continued. "The ball is round and it is designed to roll. I like to be able to use the elements and conditions. Players should have the choice of playing the ball along the ground if they want to. The little pot bunker in the middle of the first fairway is [the area] where most guys would like to leave their second shots, but they cannot because of it. Even though that bunker is only six feet wide, it is going to cause an awful lot of

The view of the second shot at the 500-yard par-5 1st hole at Doonbeg.

bother. That [feature] is straight out of St. Andrews. It was crying out to be out there."

As the crow flies, Doonbeg is approximately halfway between Ballybunion and Lahinch, looking out onto a windswept, crescent-shaped bay named Doughmore. But I give you clear warning that it will not be easy getting to this latest piece of golfing heaven even though it is less than forty miles from Shannon Airport. The roads from "civilization" to Doonbeg are pretty horrendous. (In case you've forgotten, Mr. Norman travels by helicopter.)

Perhaps if Greg had to get to Doonbeg in his beloved "bump and run" fashion along the ground, some of the enthusiasm would be knocked out of him. In a perverse way, however, the inaccessibility only adds to the charm and makes it all the more rewarding when the weary traveler arrives. Having crossed the Atlantic, I suppose an hour's journey from Shannon is not too high a price to pay—especially considering the pretty and memorable scenery one has to pass through along the way.

"I have designed the course around the 15th hole, a magnificent

*par four of 440 yards to a funnel-shaped green surrounded by the
highest dunes on the course. Landing a ball on the front edge of the
150-foot-long green, and wondering if it will stop before running
off the far end [into perdition], is far more of a challenge to me
than the target golf of hitting behind the flagstick from 187 yards
and spinning it back to six inches."*

Greg apparently does not appreciate the fact that the
vast majority of club golfers would like to be able to perform the latter feat at least once in their lives, and that they
are only going to go along with the ground ball method
accidentally! But I know what Greg means and I agree with
him. The 111-yard par-3 fourteenth is a wonderful short hole
with an amazing green site on a ledge that looms over the
beach. Having seen this hole in its embryonic state, it
frightens me every bit as much as the infamous "Calamity
Corner" (14th hole) at Royal Portrush—even though it's
only half the yardage of its Northern Ireland sister!

"What happens if you miss the green?" I asked the on-
site manager, Ed Tovey.

*Depending on the wind, the 111-yard par-3 14th will require anything
from a sand wedge to a 4-iron.*

"Reload," was his terse reply.

I can visualize somebody running out of golf balls, and on a hole measuring only 111 yards, that's unbelievable. If Greg wants to run his ball along the ground, he will have to do it on another hole.

Pretty little Doonbeg is an extraordinary place, home to only 220 souls. Or at least that was the population of this rural seaside village before Norman and his backers came along. From now on, the sky will be the limit. Nearby Lahinch, for example, has an indigenous population of 400 people that grows tenfold in the summer months. Doonbeg may suffer a similar transformation.

When Greg arrived at Shannon Airport for his first sighting early one windy morning in 1997, I am sure he was unaware of the special historical interest that the members of Limerick and Lahinch golf clubs had in the place. Doonbeg was first identified as suitable for golf as long ago as 1891 by members of the Scottish Black Watch Regiment garrisoned in Limerick City. Those fellows—along with Sir Alec Shaw, founding father and Captain and President of Limerick Golf Club—were responsible for introducing golf to the North Munster area, first at Limerick and shortly afterward at Lahinch. As soon as Limerick Golf Club was up and running successfully, this group of intrepid golfing adventurers set about finding a site for a Scottish type sea-side course that featured dunes terrain. They wanted a summer retreat where they could further indulge their new passion. Doonbeg was discovered and declared perfect by Sir Alec and his team. However, its remoteness and inac-cessibility were major and—as it turned out—insurmount-able obstacles. In those times a railway line was considered essential to the viability of any new golf facility, whether it was in Ireland, Great Britain, or America. Motorcars were not exactly ten a penny, nor were there roads fit for motor-ized vehicles. No rail line went into Doonbeg, but there was one at Lahinch, about twenty-five miles along the coast to the north. Lahinch also had a hotel that could double up as a clubhouse and headquarters.

So, Doonbeg's loss was Lahinch's gain. The economy of Lahinch has revolved around its magnificent golf links ever since. The Lahinch course was originally laid out by "Old" Tom Morris of St. Andrews for the princely fee of £4, plus expenses. The expenses may have been comparatively considerable, because I understand that Morris brought at least one of his daughters with him and they stayed for several months to oversee the work. While "Old" Tom was in the area, Sir Alec persuaded him to go to Limerick to lay out a new nine-hole course. Unfortunately, this layout was lost during one of the several location changes by the early pioneers of golf in my home city. The well researched *History of Limerick Golf Club 1891–1991* by Patrick Cotter tells fully the story of those traumatic early days as golf struggled to establish itself in Limerick and Lahinch. The book also explains the inextricable link between the two clubs.

In 1927, Dr. MacKenzie, one of the most famous golf course architects of all time, was brought over from England to redesign much of Morris's work. He also paid a visit to Limerick to lay out a new nine holes at Ballyclough. This brought the course that I call "home" up to eighteen holes for the first time. Over the years—to my chagrin—much of MacKenzie's work at Limerick was destroyed piecemeal by various club committees. Lord (of golf) forgive them, for they knew not what they did.

In 1999, under the leadership of club captain Martin Barrett, the members of Lahinch wisely decided at a specially convened Extraordinary Meeting to attempt to restore much of MacKenzie's original plans and recommendations. It is a bit of a mystery why all of MacKenzie's ideas were not incorporated at the time of his visit, but you can be sure that money was at the heart of it. The well-known and respected English architect Martin Hawtree was engaged to revive the lost spirit of MacKenzie at Lahinch in its full majesty. When the work is completed, Lahinch may at last reach its almost unlimited potential. The old girl will need to be dressed up in her finest outfit and looking her best (albeit one hundred years late) when her younger sister, Doonbeg, is ready for her debut.

I dare say "the Shark" will be paid a darn sight more than Morris and MacKenzie were paid for their design work. Plus, he is capable of matching or even surpassing their achievements, thanks to the advances in technology and knowledge now at his disposal. As Norman said, Doonbeg is perfect golfing ground. It is only a shame that the full potential of the 400-acre site could not have been exploited (in the good sense of the word). This was prevented from happening by the efforts of an environmentalist lobby that blocked the project for two years and succeeded in halting work on about one-third of the available dunes. The reason was they feared the natural habitat of a tiny, almost invisible snail by the name of *"Vertigo Angustior"* might be exterminated. If you ask me, though, this little fellow is hardy. He originated in the Ice Age and managed to survive at Lahinch for over one hundred years in spite of the best efforts of the marauding golfers there. He was declared "endangered," however, and the law is the law. Consequently, Norman and his construction crew had to find a way to work within the constraints that were handed down. I cannot believe that the golfers at Doonbeg will be any more dangerous to "Angus" than the golfers at Lahinch. If the snail has managed to survive a few miles away without any protection, why does it need the force of law to "save" it at Doonbeg? It makes no sense to me. And I am satisfied that while Norman's project will transform this part of County Clare and prove to be a superb addition to Irish links golf, the snails will remain unaffected.

"I've got the best site you've ever seen at Doonbeg in Ireland," Greg said. "The last thing I want to do is Americanize this golf course. I love links golf, and I am going to keep it as natural as I can."

❊

CHAPTER 12

A Memorable Day at Royal Troon

I have had many a great day on golf courses far and wide, but an experience at Royal Troon in 1983 ranks with the best of them. I was unable to get past the 36 holes of stroke-play qualifying and into the match-play stages of the British Amateur at Turnberry because the combined forces of the U.S. and GB&I Walker Cup teams (containing such famous names as Jay Sigel, Brad Faxon, Rick Fehr, Willie Wood, Nathaniel Crosby, Phil Parkin, and Philip Walton) pushed the standard beyond my abilities. But I did have the consolation of meeting a fellow named Curtis E. Wagner from Atlanta, Georgia, with whom I was paired during the qualifying rounds.

When Curt and I realized we were not going to make it into the match-play draw we began making plans to play golf together elsewhere in Scotland. I volunteered to go around to the R&A office, where by lucky chance I met the big boss himself, the late Keith MacKenzie, General Secretary. Friendly and helpful, he gave me a "to whom it may concern" letter of introduction pointing out that Curt and I were competitors in the Amateur Championship and he would deem it a personal favour if we were facilitated in our attempt to play some Scottish courses. We asked would this be "any good" at St. Andrews and were told we would get "preferential consideration" but no guarantees, and we would be given a guided tour of the clubhouse.

The next morning we set off for St. Andrews, but when we arrived the rain was so heavy there was no possibility whatsoever of playing golf. The greens were flooded and had to be closed for the day—a very rare occurrence. We drove back across Scotland with heavy hearts. We made a few phone calls and were given a tee time at Prestwick the following morning at 8:45. When I turned up at 7:55, the clubhouse was open but there did not seem to be anybody about. I entered and sat down in the lounge and began reading a magazine. After about ten minutes, a member of the staff came in. Politely but firmly, he told me to leave, without asking me who I was or why I was there. I was rather surprised by this and asked him why. I was told I was improperly dressed. That piece of information really stunned me because I was wearing a magnificent Pytchley Tweed Jacket that cost a small fortune, a brand new white Pringle turtleneck shirt, and cavalry twill slacks. I thought I was the absolute picture of high fashion. I was then informed that neckties must be worn at all times—day or night—in the Prestwick clubhouse. (There was no mention of trousers, by the way.) I asked if I could borrow a tie from behind the bar for ten minutes until it was time to get ready for play.

"Sorry, sir. No ties available."

I blew my stack and left in a rage. I was so cross I forgot to leave a message for Wagner. When I cooled down I drove over to Royal Troon Golf Club and was directed to the Secretary's Office. There I met Major James Montgomerie, the famous Colin's father. It was easy to see where Monty gets his sometimes "difficult" temperament: His father is of a similar disposition. Monty Senior told me that the course was booked solid for six weeks in advance and if I cared to make a reservation and come back then I could be accommodated. The R&A letter cut no ice with him. Crestfallen, and with nothing to lose, I pushed my luck. I asked if I could have permission to walk the course because I wanted to at least see the Postage Stamp hole before I went home to Ireland. Surprisingly, he agreed. "Provided," he said, "that you walk in the rough and do not disturb the golfers." I could not resist telling him that I was an international player of some experience and knew quite well how to walk a course without interfering with play, thank you very much!

When my wife Marie heard I was only going to walk the course she said she would accompany me. Royal Troon has an old style "out and in" routing. We walked all the way out to No. 8, the famous Postage Stamp, at the far end of the links, without encountering a single golfer. We dodged around a group on number nine, and then began the long walk inward. The famous eleventh hole—where Arnold Palmer trumped the field in the 1962 Open—seemed endless. As we approached the thirteenth green, which is down in a dip, we had to stop because there were four elderly gents putting. They were going about their business in a very brisk, no-nonsense manner. Before we could go past them, one of them made his way onto the fourteenth tee and hit a crisp shot down the fairway. After all four balls had been dispatched with the minimum of fuss and no little skill, I walked up to them and said:

"I am very impressed. May I introduce myself? I am the new Walker Cup selector from Ireland, and I am searching for young hidden talent. May we walk up this hole with you and study your form."

The veterans were highly amused, not least because it turned out that one of them, Alex Kyle, had been a famous Scottish champion and Walker Cup player many years earlier. These fellows were no "spring chickens," but they could still play. We had a great chat between shots, and they listened sympathetically when Marie told them of my litany of disappointments. When we reached the seventeenth green we decided there was no point in making the long walk back to the eighteenth tee and that we should leave and be on our way. We had gone about a hundred yards when we heard a loud whistle. The old boys were waving us to come back. Russell McCreath was their spokesman and he said:

"We had a wee chat and were wondering if you will be around tomorrow? We are playing at 9 o'clock sharp in the morning and Alex says you can have his place. We are all former Captains of the club and you will be our guest."

I was delighted. We had planned to drive south to the Lake District that evening for a few days, but we immediately postponed that. We met the next morning and my green fees were waived. I was invited to play off the Open Championship tees, a rare honour, and my hosts said they would play off the members' tees. It would be a level match, I was told—me against the best ball of the other three—and there would be the usual "wee wager."

"What might that be?" I asked, slightly concerned.

"We always play for five," Duncan Lodge told me.

That was fine by me. Green fees were fifteen pounds, so I would still come out even for the day, I thought. Those canny Scots were easily worth £5 a man to me. Off we went, and to make a long story short I played close to my best, making a regulation par at the Postage Stamp and a birdie at the long eleventh, and finally sank a tricky four-footer for a par on the last green to be around in 73 blows to win the match by one hole. I was delighted. Marie and I were escorted into the clubhouse for tea and sandwiches, and then (with much ceremony) I was presented with a shilling piece (5p) by each of the vanquished. This was either the exchange rate gone mad or another example of Scottish frugality. But I did not care. I had just had a hugely enjoyable round of golf on a historic course. Proudly, Russell McCreath insisted on showing me his locker. It had Arnold Palmer's nameplate on it because Arnie had used it when he won the Open in 1962. Then Duncan whispered to me, "I bet you would like to go around again."

I said I would, if it was okay with Marie. Not for the first time, Marie had her priorities right and she gave the go-ahead. Duncan said he would not be able to manage another round but he would play the first hole with me and then retire. If I was approached, I should say that I had been playing with him but that he had been called away unexpectedly. I had just said my final goodbye when who loomed into view but Curt Wagner! Somehow he had managed to wangle a tee time for the two of us. However, my hasty departure from Prestwick upset his secret plan to surprise me. He thought I had gone home to Ireland. Once more we joined forces, and had a free run on an almost empty golf course. Curt had a caddie with him who had worked for Aoki in the Open Championship. We had great fun listening to his stories. I do not think I ever had a more enjoyable day in my whole life.

Epilogue
Russell McCreath is now a sprightly ninety years-old and rain or shine he continues to play nine holes of golf every day at Troon. "Still searching for the secret," he told me when I tracked him down at Christmas 2000.

❀

CHAPTER 13

Heroes and All-Time Favourites

"Slammin" Sam Snead

As far as the golf explosion in Ireland was concerned, 1960 was a pivotal year. And Slammin' Sam was deeply involved with it. The Canada Cup (which was to become known as the World Cup of Golf) came to Ireland for the first time that year. It is an event for two-man teams representing their country. Portmarnock drew unprecedented crowds, but there was intense countrywide interest as well. Arnold Palmer and Sam Snead from the U.S. were the main attractions. The Americans won, of course, but Flory Van Donck from Belgium pushed Snead into second place in the individual competition. This was possibly an early warning of the burgeoning talents of mainland Europeans.

On account of this visit to Ireland, Sam Snead became my first golfing hero. I had not become an addict yet, but the golf disease was incubating and about to break out. The pictures of Sam in his exotic straw hat and stories about the distances he could hit the ball were inspiring. Enthusiastic eyewitness reports on Sam's prodigious and stylish play fanned the flames of desire out of control and I was hooked. Father Enright gave me a little paperback book titled *Power Golf* containing drawings of Sam in every conceivable position during the swing and it became my bible.

My mother had a tailor's mirror in her bedroom that was perfect for me to pose in front of as I tried to imitate Sam's posture, setup and motions. On one disastrous occasion I could not resist the temptation to take a full-blooded swing while "admiring" myself, and a huge divot was gouged out of the carpet. There was hell to pay. A promising golf career could have been snuffed out then and there. I tried to make up for the damage caused with "free" lessons and swing tips for the rest of my mother's golfing life. Her two Captain's Prize wins are proof that my contributions helped, I suppose.

Sam Snead's magnificent swing was widely regarded as the most elegant ever. I saw Sam play "in the flesh" several times, but only got the chance to study him closely when he played in the 1970 Kerrygold Classic at Waterville, when he was fifty-eight years old. Even at that age he was top class. Sam's exceptional athleticism was the reason why he was so good and lasted so long—he won more PGA Tour events (82) than anyone in history and, until Tiger came along, it seemed unlikely that his record would ever be broken. His swing was so comfortable-looking, it would have been easy to absorb and replicate. If a young fellow with athletic ability could have played golf with Sam every day for a month, simply by copying the great man's style and rhythm he would have been able to play off scratch in no time.

I managed to have a short conversation with my hero once. It was in the upstairs "loo" of the Augusta National clubhouse. There I was doing my business, when who pops into the urinal alongside? None other than Slammin' Sam!

"Hey pro, whaddya shoot?" he says to me. I was astonished to be addressed in such a manner by one of the all-time stars of golf.

"You were not in such high spirits the last time I saw you," says I.

"Where was that?"

"The Kerrygold Classic, Waterville, Ireland."

"Shoot, man," says Sam, "does it ever stop raining in that goddamned country? But tell me, how is "Himself" swinging these days?"

(If you do not know who "Himself" is, read on!)

I did not have the heart to tell Sam that he had the whole of Ireland talking about him for the wrong reasons at Waterville. Back then, covering live golf was still a bit of an unknown quantity for Irish Television (RTE). Their broadcasters had minimal golf expertise. Brendan O'Reilly, the former Irish Olympic athlete from Michigan State University, was dispatched with a camera crew to the nether regions of County Kerry. Saturday was a glorious day, but Sunday was brutal. The show opened up with a picture of the barely visible eighteenth green due to the thick fog and horizontal rain. The next picture shown to the audience at home was a head and shoulders shot of a saturated Sam Snead. Such a picture of misery! He was wearing a bright red hat and the rain had caused the red dye to trickle down his face, creating the most awful apparition. It looked like blood.

"How did you play today, Sam?" O'Reilly asked.

"Lousy."

"How did you enjoy the course, and playing in Ireland?"

"Crap!"

"Sam, you were playing with Dr. Michael Dargan, president of Aer Lingus. How did Dr. Dargan play?"

"He could not scratch his arse with a rake."

Cut. TV screen quickly goes black. Somebody had pulled the plug before the conversation deteriorated any further. As you can imagine, it made a big impact and got the viewers talking. I still think Sam is the greatest, and his little dance on Swilican Bridge at St. Andrews in 2000 only reinforced my admiration.

"Himself" — Christy O'Connor Sr.

Christy O'Connor Junior, known throughout Ireland as "the nephew," had a highly successful first season on the Senior PGA Tour in America in 1999. This happened when he might more realistically have expected to have been working all-out on his golf course design business at home in Ireland. Instead, Junior was in America winning more money in a year than his illustrious uncle, Christy Senior, was able to win in a long and highly successful career, which contained more wins and distinctions than Junior ever enjoyed. Furthermore, "the nephew" seems to have achieved more fame with one shot at the conclusion of the 1989 Ryder Cup at the Belfry than Senior managed in his ten Ryder Cup appearances. That is the fickle way of fame and fortune. It is possible to win more money in one tournament these days than in the entire lifetime of a Hogan, Nelson, Snead, or O'Connor Senior.

Impressed and all as I am by Christy Junior's exploits, it is my unshakeable view that O'Connor Senior, affectionately known as "Himself," is the greatest Irish golfer that ever lived. Christy never won the big one, the British Open (as another Irishman, Fred Daly, did in 1947 at Hoylake), but he was a master shot-maker with nerves of steel. He also had the knack of being able to pick up record paychecks. Unfortunately, those paychecks were only a pittance by today's standards. He was the first European player to win a four-figure prize (in 1955) at a time when a modest house could be built for the same sum.

To watch Christy hit drivers off the turf or long irons into the wind was an awesome sight. He was a magician with the wedge and holed as many long putts as anyone who played the game. When he was preparing for the Irish Professional Close Championship in 1973 at my home club, I was invited to play a game with him. It cost me a side wager of £10 — half a week's wages at the time — but it was money well spent to be able to study a master at work. Playing "out of my skin" on the first nine, I went out in 33 to be 2 up. But you could see Christy changing gears on the tenth tee as he decided it was time to give this kid the brush-off. On the way back his 32 outclassed my 36.

I was thrilled to be at Woodbrook when Christy won the

Christy Sr. at play in the 2000 J.P. McManus Pro-Am Classic. (Tony Rodgers)

Carroll's International Tournament, the forerunner of the resurrected Irish Open. When "Himself" went on a roll in those days, the murmurs and excitement around the course were electric. It is a shame that Christy is not better known in America. Had he accepted any of the eighteen invitations he received from the Masters Committee at Augusta, he could have been. But he felt the journey was too daunting, the April timing was not right, and the rewards inappropriate to the cost involved. Billy Casper once said that it was lucky for Palmer and Nicklaus that Christy was not born in America because they would not have won as often.

Christy came close to winning the British Open on a number of occasions. The nearest miss was at Lytham in 1958. If he had made a par at the final hole he would have joined Peter Thomson (the winner) and Dave Thomas in a playoff. Both were playing several groups behind him and unfortunately it was not known exactly what was required to win or tie. After driving into one of the nasty pot bunkers that litter the eighteenth hole at Lytham, Christy—with no "back off" in his nature—went for the green. He failed to extricate himself at the first attempt and it cost him a double-bogey. Half an hour later Thomson drove into the same trap, played out backwards and then got down in two more shots for his par. If only Christy had done likewise, his reputation might have been secure for all time.

In 1970, Christy won a huge world record–breaking check of £25,000 in the John Player Classic at Nottingham. Once more he bunkered his final tee shot, but this time he did know the score and what was needed to beat Tony Jacklin. Ignoring the Lytham experience, he hit a tremendous long iron onto the green and two-putted. The celebrations continued long into the night and for several days afterward, so that when Christy arrived in Ballybunion for a *Shell's Wonderful World of Golf* challenge against American Bob Goalby, he was a bit the worse for wear. To add further spice, there was no love lost between these two. A few years earlier, during a Ryder Cup match in America, Christy had missed the GB&I team bus back to the hotel. Since the Americans had courtesy cars, Christy asked Goalby for a ride. Bob took offence when Christy lit a cigarette in his car. A few heated words were exchanged and the aggravation was carried onto the course the next day when they were drawn to play each other. O'Connor won that match, but when Goalby saw the condition Christy was in after all the celebrating in Nottingham, he thought he saw an opportunity. He suggested that the winner should take the entire Shell purse. Christy, with £25,000 already in his pocket, accepted. It turned out to be an atrocious day. The cold and the wind were not long in clearing Christy's hangover. The high wind suited the Galway man and the American was blown away by a combination of the elements and Christy's skill.

Now well into his seventies, Christy beats his age as regularly as clockwork. He did yet again at the J.P. McManus Pro–Am at Limerick in July of 2000, with Tiger Woods playing in the group ahead of him.

Ben Hogan — Mr. Harrumph!

Back in the 1940s, before the age of golf millionaires and superstars, the travelling troupe that earned its living following the sun playing golf used to gravitate to the Dunedin Country Club, a little bit north of Clearwater in Florida, during the winter off-season. Ben Hogan may have been one of the star players at the time, but he lived more or less the same lifestyle as everyone else. He travelled around the country in his car, not his Learjet. Relative to his fellow players, the life-style was similar; he merely had more money in the bank, that is all. He still spent all day every day at the golf club hitting balls on the range, eating, drinking, and playing cards. That was the way of life back then. At Dunedin, the players played for their own money on the course and off it. Hogan, in spite of his surly reputation, was one of the boys. He would hang around the club and play with anyone, as long as they had a wad of notes.

A young, ambitious, well-bankrolled golfer who had just joined the PGA Tour rolled into town. His name was Al Bessilink. He was like a lot of young men in a hurry to the top. He watched Hogan from a safe distance, admiring his play and wondering how he could befriend the rather stern older man. Al felt certain that if he could play a round or two with Ben he would pick up some useful tips that would help him on his way. Eventually, he found the courage to make an approach.

"Any chance of a game with you, Mr. Hogan?" Bessilink asked.

"I don't play for less than $1,000."

A game was arranged, and Hogan, not unsurprisingly, clobbered the young man. Al was most disappointed that their conversation during the round had been nearly non-existent. He had gotten bad value.

Maybe he had something on his mind, thought Bessilink.

They played again. Same result. And again they played. Al's bankroll was dwindling fast.

"Mr. Hogan, can we have another game tomorrow, and will you give me a chance to win some of my money back?"

"Sure kid. What do you want to play for?"

"I thought $2,000, and will you give me a couple of strokes? One a side, perhaps?"

"Sonny, if you want strokes you better go home. This is the PGA Tour." Harrumph!

Not many Irishmen have been blessed with the opportunity to watch Ben Hogan play in the flesh. He only played in the United Kingdom twice, and never in Ireland. Roland Stafford had told me before I went to Augusta in 1966 that I should not waste my time watching Nicklaus or Palmer. Instead, I was to concentrate on studying Hogan. I followed Roland's advice and it was an unforgettable experience. Hogan had an aura about him that was almost mystical. Everything about him was immaculate: his clothing, his demeanour, even the way he smoked his cigarette.

When I was in college in Florida in 1965–1966, I persuaded my father, who was owner and publisher of the *Limerick Weekly Echo* newspaper, to apply for a 1966 Masters Press Badge for his golf correspondent (me). It worked. On the first day, Hogan was paired with Michael Bonnallack, the reigning British Amateur Champion. I followed them around every step of the way. In 1979, Bonnallack was forced to come down from such lofty heights and back to the reality of being paired with me in the English Amateur Open at Little Aston. I asked Michael if Hogan had said anything of note to him during their game together.

"Not really. Just the odd grunt here and there," was the reply.

Hogan's swing was not a thing of beauty. But the way the ball flew off the clubface was. Every shot had the same trajectory, and it was fast. I clearly remember how tight everything in his action seemed to be. He jammed his elbows tight to his chest, and he maintained the straightest left arm I ever saw.

All these years later my abiding memory is not of any particular shot I saw him play, but the hair-raising emotion I felt as I watched him struggle up the steep hill to the eighteenth green at the end of his second round in the company of Arnold Palmer. What a contrast in styles there was between those two.

Nicklaus was the holder of the Masters that year, and he went on to repeat after a playoff. The extra round cost me the tee time I had won in the Press Lottery to play the course on Monday. I have never forgiven Gay Brewer for three-putting the final green to bring that playoff about.

Gary Player—The Black Knight

"You must have great golfers in Ireland," said the wee man in black to the rather surprised and taken aback group of reporters waiting to interview him after one of his typically energetic practice sessions before the Irish Open at Portmarnock some years ago.

"Why do you say that, Gary?"

"Well, anytime I come to Ireland I never see anybody working on their games on the practice ground. Obviously they are so good they do not need to practice!"

That is so typical of Gary Player, one of my earliest golf heroes. My regard for him has lasted a lifetime. He was a particularly good one to admire because he is never lost for words and always has interesting and stimulating things to say. He gives such fabulous interviews that I am sure he must rehearse in advance. Gary trains his body in a way that was once unheard of for a golfer. While playing he is constantly stretching his muscles and exercising. He watches his diet. Although he often wears black clothes, he is a highly colourful personality who knows he is a performer. He is prepared to give full value on and off the course. Gary has been a tremendous salesman for golf throughout his career.

He used to have a terrific little syndicated cartoon strip

in the *Sunday Express* that created many a discussion at our dinner table. To give you an idea of what it was like in our house at meal times, my mother put a notice on the kitchen door that read "Golf Spoken Here." My brother Brien, feeling this was not quite accurate, added "only" in the appropriate spot. That was about it at 14 Shannon Drive when we were growing up, and it has carried on that way ever since.

Father Enright "adored" Gary Player, mainly because he also was a fitness fanatic. Enright said Gary got more out of his God-given talents than anyone else ever did, achieving "the maximum with the minimum." He thought so highly of the little South African that he eulogised him to such an extent in his Sunday sermon at Mary on the Hill Parish Church in Augusta in 1981 that you would have been forgiven for thinking we were attending the man's obsequies. The congregation was delighted and thought the visiting Irish priest had gone out of his way to prepare a suitable theme for Masters week. It certainly made a change from normal sermons. Not a bit of it. A homily about golf and Gary Player came easily to Father Gerry.

Player is still going as strong as ever in 2001, forty-two years after he won his first major. Every time he makes one of his pronouncements, I listen with the greatest interest.

Gary has made several marvellous instructional films. Noel Harris and Nick McMahon showed many of them in the clubhouse at Ballyclough, back in the era of *Shell's Wonderful World of Golf.* One key phrase of his still rings in my ears: "Park your hands in the garage!"

That concept has always helped me, and does so more and more as I get older. It is an easy swing thought for the young and limber, but one that is more important than ever when your athleticism and flexibility are not what they used to be.

Gary's sand play is legendary, but the rest of his short game isn't bad either. I remember travelling to the Irish Open at Portmarnock with the sole intention of studying how Gary went about building a score. It was most enlightening. His striking was not very good (he was fighting a destructive hook) but I was mesmerised by his recovery play and positive attitude. He turned a possible 80 into a respectable 71, thanks to an array of short-game shots. Run-ups, floaters, and skidders were all on show. Gary fully deserves to be recognised as one of the greatest players of all time because his record and longevity speak for themselves. Perhaps his greatest achievement was winning the U.S. Open in 1965, accomplished with a dreadful set of prototype aluminium-shafted irons. The equipment had to have been a huge handicap, but he won in spite of it.

I am not a big man myself but I was surprised to find myself towering over him when I met Gary in the Augusta National clubhouse. He called me "Sir," which I found highly amusing, and he was in no rush to get away from my small talk. He also gave me a dreaded blow-by-blow account of his round earlier that day, perhaps because he saw my media badge and felt obliged. His enthusiastic approach to life is so inspiring it struck me that he could easily have been a successful evangelist or politician.

I asked him about his fitness regime. He told me with some passion that he had to exercise in order to make himself strong enough to be able to hit the ball as far as Nicklaus and Palmer. He then gave me a blisteringly sincere sermon about the way a sportsman should take care of his body. I had heard similar words many times from Father Enright.

"It is becoming increasingly necessary for a golfer to train and diet sensibly if they want to compete at the highest level. Alcohol should only be indulged in very sparingly, if at all," said Gary. He is correct, of course. This approach becomes more vital with every passing year as the competition grows ever more fierce. Gary went on to say that any golfer who has dominated the game for a period has been an exceptionally long ball hitter. As equipment has improved, all players are longer now. But the top players are dramatically longer. It is how they separate themselves from the pack. Hitting straight is taken for granted, but hitting long is not. The only way to achieve this is to make yourself fitter, more flexible, and stronger. Gary Player has impeccably followed his own advice throughout his long and brilliant career.

"The Brad" — Harry Bradshaw

Harry Bradshaw may have been a great player, but he was an even better raconteur. It seemed as if he could recall every shot he ever played and was the most wonderful company on the links, whether playing for a few "bob" or giving a lesson. Harry should have won the British Open at Royal St. George's in 1949, only for an unfortunate incident with a broken bottle. It seems incredible in this day and age that

Harry Bradshaw.

there were no officials in the vicinity to give him the free drop to which he was entitled. Harry wasted a stroke breaking a bottle that his golf ball had somehow come to rest in and then played on regardless. It is also worth remembering that in 1949 there was also a 36-hole qualifying tournament, in which everyone had to take part. Harry led this, so for six rounds he was in the lead. Bobby Locke, however, tied him and then beat him in a 36-hole playoff. Winner and runner-up played eight rounds of highly competitive golf that week.

Recognised as a genius on and around the greens, Harry employed an exaggerated head down mode. His amazing ability in this department of the game was directly linked to a constant practise regime and the eccentricity of another Reverend mentor, a Father Gleeson, who used to play with his young protégé at Delgany. Harry was not allowed to go to the next tee until he had sunk his putt from wherever his ball had landed on the green. The famous "Holy Office" would be produced and the priest would sit down beside the green and refuse to budge until the putt was holed. It did not take Harry long to figure out that the nearer to the hole he hit his ball the sooner he would be out of there and on to the next hole. It was a great incentive to improve approach play as well as putting.

I received several lessons from Harry myself, and everything he told me has stood the test of time. One of the best bits of advice he gave me was not exactly appreciated at the time, but I grew to learn how right he was. I asked him to tell me what single piece of advice he would give himself if he could turn the clock back. With typical simplicity he said, "Mind me poor old feet!"

He also told me that the secret to becoming a good putter was to practise for twenty minutes every day with two balls, rolling one up against the other from all distances and angles, and imagining every putt was for "something." If you cannot get onto a green, "putt on the carpet at home," I was told. Henry Longhurst once described Harry's swing as agricultural, but he was a very straight hitter who rarely left the fairway. That is all that matters, because golf is not a beauty contest. "The Brad" attributed his straight hitting to an unusual grip, which he devised himself. He scorned the orthodox Vardon grip and overlapped the last three fingers of his right hand on top of his left in order to eliminate the tendency to overpower the club with the stronger hand. Harry knew how to score. "Learn to turn three shots into two," he declared, "and nobody will beat you."

His uncanny ability to score low can be traced back to the way he began his professional career at Kilcroney as a teenager. He had a regular Tuesday appointment to play with a wealthy, elderly lady member, a Mrs. Hayes, who used to pay Harry five shillings for every birdie he made during their rounds together. One day Harry failed to birdie any hole on the front nine. His benefactor teased him on the way to the tenth tee by saying, "You are not trying, Harry!"

Harry promptly made three birdies in a row, suffered a lip-out at No. 13, and then birdied the last five holes on the trot! Harry's eyes were bulging with delight when he was handed two crispy pound notes, a sum of money not to be sneezed at during the depressed 1930s.

There are legions of stories about Harry's reputation for stinginess. For example, back in the early 1970s, when decimalization was introduced, Harry unwittingly found himself the owner of a jarful of useless halfpennies. My friend Michael Galvin needed a ball marker and entered Harry's "emporium" to purchase one.

"Can I have a marker please, Harry?"

Whereupon Harry handed over a no-longer-legal halfpenny coin. "This is what they are using for markers these days," he told Michael.

"How much do I owe you?"

"Ten pence," says Harry.

That is one of the most ingenious ways of multiplying money that I ever heard.

He could be kind, too. Galvin told me that when he was

a university member at Portmarnock, Harry used to charge the member's £1 for a round of golf. But if three students could rustle up 6/8d. each (33p.), he would happily play a round with them and was fulsome with his advice and swing tips. I have to say that on my trips to him for lessons, which were supposed to be of one hour's duration, he was not a clock-watcher. Once he spent three and a half delightful hours with me and would not take a penny more than the fee originally agreed. On another occasion he cut my lesson short and offered me the chance of "double or nothing" by taking me onto the links for a match. I was one up after eight holes. But from the ninth to the eighteenth, Harry had only nine putts—one-putting every green and holing a pitch shot to beat me! A valuable but expensive lesson.

Harry never conceded strokes, preferring to give "holes up." He liked to concede any advantage by declaring a deficit of say, two down, on the first tee and then went into battle without the need to give up strokes. Sometimes he might have the lead whittled away to nothing after a few holes. He had it gauged that he would go around Portmarnock in 70 every time, certainly six times out of ten, and two of the others might be in the sixties. Not many amateurs could match that. He ignored the designated tee-ing ground so that he always played a course that fitted him exactly. His excuses for doing so were ingenious, but he was such fun to play with that nobody cared. He gave excellent value for the few pounds he won from ninety-five percent of the golfing population who entered his spider's web.

Sir Henry and Jake

Father Gerry Enright had close friendships with both the legendary Irish golfer Harry Bradshaw and the illustrious Englishman Sir Henry Cotton. He often travelled to tour-naments to watch them in action, and later in life regularly went to Penina, Portugal, on holiday, where he played golf with Cotton and his wife Toots, a former lady champion of

Sir Henry Cotton, 3-time winner of the Open Championship ('34, '37, '48), with Fred Daly in attendance, demonstates some of his favorite drills in 1987. (Golfer's Companion)

Argentina. The Cottons were devout Catholics and liked the company of priests. A private Mass was reciprocated for the courtesy of the course and an occasional game with the great man. Enthusiastic stories about the deeds of Bradshaw and Cotton helped to fire my imagination.

It is sometimes forgotten what a dominant figure Henry Cotton was back in 1930s and 1940s. He was the Faldo of his day, head and shoulders above his contemporaries. He was such a confident and suave character that on his own he changed the servile attitude of professional golfers in Britain. He was a fashion-conscious trailblazer who exploited the media, writing articles and making instructional films that were shown in cinemas. It was the first time that golf was being taught in Britain in a structured and systematic way. Until then, all coaching was individualistic and "hit or miss"—if you will excuse the pun. Henry believed "educated hands" were the secret to good golf, and he trained his by hitting against an automobile tire, mimicking the impact position as he struck the clubface against the tire.

Just about the time that I began to play, the Golfing Union of Ireland started a Youth Coaching Policy with a genial Ulster man (almost a contradiction in terms) named Tom Montgomery at the helm. I was among the first to benefit, and Eddie Hackett was employed to coach a small group of elite young players from each of the four provinces of Ireland. Eddie had worked as an assistant to Henry Cotton at Temple Golf Club in England and was a dedicated disciple of Henry's theories, which he followed slavishly but not with much imagination. Later Hackett found his niche and became Ireland's most prolific golf architect, but as a swing coach he was not very good. The GUI was doing the right thing but it had put the wrong person in charge.

Then John Jacobs came along in the mid-1960s to lead the development of golf instruction in Britain and Ireland. Jacobs applied the laws of physics to golf. By watching the flight of the ball, John could work out everything he needed to know about his pupil's swing. He traced everything back to the path direction of the clubhead as it passed through the ball and the angle of the clubface when it made contact. It sounds simple, but anyone who tackles the technique of the golf swing from this point of reference cannot go wrong. When Eddie Hackett retired, Jacobs was brought over by the GUI for a number of intensive coaching sessions. Sitting behind a screen, unable to see the player, he could say what was right or wrong by listening to the sound of the strike and watching the flight of the ball. I thought this was bordering on witchcraft at the time. He told his pupils that the "behaviour" of the golf ball is determined by four, and only four, impact factors interacting with one another:

1. The direction in which the club faces "looks," or points.

2. The direction (path) in which the clubhead travels.

3. The angle at which the clubhead arrives at the ball (angle of attack).

4. The speed of the clubhead at impact.

Getting these elements right is much easier said than done. If you can understand them, however, you are well on the way to playing better golf as long as you do not think too much about it while on the golf course. These matters are for consideration on the practice ground only. Paradoxically, if you spend too much time ball watching on the practice ground when you are working on your swing, you will never improve because you will be so discouraged. Instead, lots of practise drills without the ball, in front of a mirror or a video camera, will do the trick. It cannot be emphasised enough how much of a distraction the ball is if you are trying to change your technique. That is the priceless lesson I learned from John Jacobs all those years ago.

❋

Chapter 14

The Great John Burke
King of Lahinch

Long before I took up golf, my Dad told me—with great reverence—colourful stories about a man whom he always referred to as "the great John Burke." When I began playing at Lahinch, this mystery man's reputation seemed to grow and grow. At Lahinch, Burke was called The King of the Links. This was slightly ironic, because John was a proud Old Irish Republican Army man who had served during the difficult times of the 1920s, when Ireland was struggling to secure its independence from British rule. Naturally, in the circumstances, he had little time for royalty of any sort. In fact, John's association with the IRA cost him his place on the Walker Cup team when his freedom-fighting past accidentally became known to the British golf establishment. He told me this himself, more with pride than bitterness. It was the era of Eric Fiddian and Cyril Tolley, but John was by far the best player in these islands. Apart from his single appearance in 1932, the Walker Cup selectors ignored him. It was a complete travesty of justice.

How the British found out about John's politics was interesting. During a raid on a British Army Encampment in County Cork, John's brigade "purloined" a fine pair of brown military boots belonging to an enemy officer, amongst other goodies. The boots had the initials "JB" displayed prominently on them, so they were given to John as a matter of course. Some weeks later John and a few colleagues were detained for questioning in County Clare. Gradually it dawned on him that the Interrogating Officer was the owner of the very boots he was wearing. It could have been disastrous if it had been discovered. Fortunately for him, a most uncomfortable few hours passed by without the boots being noticed.

Exactly ten years later John was playing for Ireland against England at Sandwich, south of London. During one of his rounds, he became aware of a familiar face in the crowd but could not place it. After the game he approached the gentleman who had aroused his curiosity only to find that it was the officer whose boots had been "captured," and who had questioned him about his IRA membership. When the secret of the boots was revealed, the officer fell about laughing and "forgave" John with alacrity. Soon afterward, John was selected to play for Great Britain & Ireland in the Walker Cup matches in America. The team was to sail on the "Queen Mary" from Southampton, with the Irish contingent joining the boat at Cobh, County Cork en route. John's new friend, not realizing this, drove to Southampton to wish him bon voyage. But of course, John was not there. Instead, the former officer told one of the GB&I officials about his and John's unusual friendship and gave him a handwritten "best of luck" note for John. When the note was being handed over, John was told in no uncertain terms that it would be his last Walker Cup because there was "no place on a British team for IRA terrorists." Treated as persona non grata by his colleagues throughout the trip, John decided, for a bit of devilment, to play up his Irish Nationalism by refusing to honour "God Save the King." He also insisted on his separate Irish identity being recognized at every opportunity. Having been told he was never going to be selected again, he got as much enjoyment as he could tweaking British tails in this harmless way. But it cost him.

At Lahinch, John's royal status was fully justified on account of his record of winning the annual South of Ireland Championship on eleven occasions, and indeed he was "discouraged" from entering the championship for a number of years because his presence was affecting the size and quality of the field. The revenue was badly needed by the club. Being a local boy, born close to the Village of Lahinch in 1899, John was well aware of the importance of "the South" competition to the well-being of the golf club and the developing economy of the village, so he complied. Only Joe Carr has won more Irish and Provincial Championships than

At Lahinch, Burke was known as "The King of the Links."

John Burke. It should be remembered, though, that World War II interfered with John's run of victories. No wonder the locals are still proud of their great champion long after his death in 1974.

As a young man, John spent some time as a caddie. But when he showed promise and a talent for the game, a far-seeing member who had observed his magnificent, flowing action when playing illegally on the links in the evenings with his pal, local butcher Mick O'Loughlin, kindly championed a campaign to have them both invited to join the club. They were the first locals to be so honoured. The two friends set about taking full advantage of the compliment and were determined to master the game. Together they undertook a methodical and scientific approach. Burke's stated credo, which he passed on to me years later, was, "Good, better, best. Do not rest until your good is better than your best."

It should also be remembered that John played during the Bobby Jones era, a time when amateur golf was considered more important than the professional game. When I asked him why he never turned professional, he said he could make more money and have a better life by remaining amateur. That would not be so today, but back then it was the case.

A master of improvisation, John learned the game by experimenting with every shot and situation imaginable with a limited arsenal of implements, just like Ballesteros many years later at Pedrena. John worked hard and eventually thought he might be ready to begin competing, so he applied for a handicap. Straight off he was given scratch, and he maintained that standard for all of his golfing life. Even after he acquired a full set of clubs, John continued to play a game that featured all sorts of made-up shots. Consequently, his repertoire included an array of trick shots. The famous trick shot artist Joe Kirkwood wanted John to join him on one of his World Tours when he saw what John could do during his visit to Limerick in 1937.

John was a character and a loveable rogue. Long before the balata ball was ever heard of, he talked me into having what he termed a "soft" ball available for use at short holes. He suggested I tee the ball a little higher than usual so that the weaker top section of the blade would make contact. One could then play a much stronger club than was really needed, deliberately show the club to one's opponent, putting on a show of throwing grass in the air to gauge the wind and discussing the shot out loud in an effort to mislead the gullible! When I tried this tactic myself, it achieved inconsistent results and I was not long abandoning it, preferring to play my own game and not become too embroiled with the opposition. Another trick he told me was to throw the ball down onto the ground, spurning the use of a peg. If the ball sat up nicely for a brassie, as he called it, fire away, but if the ball rolled into a poor lie, not to be too proud to pick it up and tee it properly. Such "one-upmanships" were designed to unsettle the enemy in the middle of a match. John also told me that whenever I was in a tight situation, to walk to the shorter ball at some stage and claim it and hope that my opponent would go to the longer ball only to have the humbling experience of having to walk back. John was full of such roguery. He played that way all of his life; for him it was all part of the enjoyment. Father Enright told two stories about John that emphasise his impish attitude. Once, John bet the Reverend a "half a crown" that he would not get down in two putts. When my friend one-putted, Burke claimed that Father Enright had lost the bet. On another occasion John threw a coin into a bunker beside Father Enright's ball. When Father Gerry stooped to pick up the money, a penalty was called for touching the sand! In spite of this carry on, Father Gerry thought the world of John Burke and was in awe of his ability.

My own first experience of this phantom King of the Links occurred about the time I began playing in major competitions like the Castletroy Scratch Cup and "the South" at Lahinch. John, who had become stricken by multiple sclerosis and was confined to a wheelchair, had a dispensation allowing him to be driven onto the golf course in his car, so that he could follow the golfers around. There was always a wave of expectation when Burke's car loomed into view. It was considered a great honour if he followed you for a few holes and spoke to you in the process. I was not long back in Limerick after my American college adventure when I was delighted to receive a phone call from the man himself summoning me to come to his home. To give himself something to do, John had built a small wooden hut at the side of his house on Lelia Street, rigged up a net, and began giving lessons while sitting in his wheelchair. It was his way of keeping in touch with the game, current players, and events. He was clearly more interested in the chat than any money he might have earned. I was invited to hit a few balls so that my potential could be assessed. I was very flattered. Gradually we became good

friends. Although my golf exploits fell short of our expectations, it was not for lack of effort. We had a lot of fun in
the process and I kept him amused with some dramatic
excuses for not doing better.

John was a good teacher and it was not entirely his fault
I did not succeed in winning the Irish National Amateur
Championship, which was what he wanted me to do more
than anything. Under his guidance, John had me hitting the
ball as well as anyone in the country for short, sporadic
bursts. Neither of us could understand why I was so inconsistent. I was inclined to believe the "bad publicity" that
was promulgated about me by golf officials who really did
not have a clue. They condemned me for having "a brittle
temperament." It was an easy way to rationalize failure, and
it may have appeared to be that way on the surface, but I
was a lot tougher and more in control than I was credited.
I know now my so-called "great swing" was faulty, and
nobody was able to see that. It was pretty rather than effective. If I had achieved what I did in the game with an ugly
swing, I would have received more recognition and respect.
Instead, I was deemed "a disappointment."

Burke taught me to hang a tee peg in his golf net and
asked me to strike it with the ball in order to teach me how
to control trajectory, which is the key to the art of distance
control. When I asked him how I could hit the ball further,
he simply said, "Hit it purer and higher." Together we
developed practice routines that broke the monotony of
hitting hundreds of balls into a net. Imaginary rounds of
golf on various courses were "played." John called the shots,
announced the prevailing conditions, warned about hazards, etc. He then assessed the strike, declared a "result"
and told me what to do next. There are computerized
screens for playing such games these days, but we did it all
in our imaginations. We made it as realistic as possible.
Every conceivable shot was practised. It was a tremendous
exercise in concentration and visualisation. I find myself
coaching my teenaged nephew, Simon Morris, in a similar

manner these days. It is clear from the expression on his face that he enjoys it.

At the time that John was coaching me, I was very fiery and overly sensitive to criticism. But he used to roast me regardless because of my "lack of success," as he defined it. Only once did we have a falling out. We had a hot debate over the correct chipping and pitching action. I believed in firm wrists and a kind of a shoulder-rocking pendulum stroke called "triangle, track, and target" that I learned from Roland Stafford. John advocated a handsy method, featuring a long backswing and a truncated follow-through. The row grew hot and heavy until John wailed, "I wish I could get out of this bloody chair and show you!" That was upsetting, that this great man who had been struck down by a horrible disease could not stand up to demonstrate what he once could have done blindfolded.

To my later regret, I completely believed in John Burke's swing training methods. But before going into some of his theories, I would like to tell you one of *his* favourite stories. It concerns Henry Cotton when he came to Ireland on one of his coaching tours for the GUI. As usual, an elite squad of players was sent to the great man.

"Try a swing," Cotton said to one of the hopefuls.

The player obliged.

"Try again." The player obliged.

"And again." The player did it again.

"Now," Cotton said, "I want you to swing as if you were about to hit the ball."

The player did what he was told.

"What is your handicap?" Cotton asked.

"Scratch at a seaside links in the west of Ireland," was the proud reply.

Cotton was surprised. "You must be a hell of a great putter!" he said.

John always enjoyed telling that tale.

Being able to develop a swing that will stand up to the pressure of competition eludes many good players. When confidence and concentration are disturbed, as they inevitably will be in an event that takes several days to complete, very few have a sound enough swing to carry them through. A player's ability to progress is essentially determined by his technique. John maintained it was imperative to get everything to work in unison. This helps to create rhythm, timing, power, and a balanced action that would repeat no matter what the circumstances.

Here is a summary of John Burke's dictums:

1. Grip the club very lightly with both palms facing each other. (He was not fussy how you might interlock the fingers, if you did it at all.)

2. Try to build a flowing, relaxed action through practise, maintaining the same even-paced swing speed back and forward.

3. Concentrate on being able to hold a balanced finish after each shot. Never stumble or recoil. He would poke you in the ribs with his walking stick on reaching the finish of the swing, to see if you would lose balance.

4. The start of your backswing and downswing should never be hurried.

5. Never sway. Imagine your right leg is a pole and swing around it.

6. Never stretch at address or during the swing. (He scoffed at the idea of a stiff, straight left arm.)

7. Never hit blindly. Always take careful aim at something. (Legendary instructor Harvey Penick said something similar: "Take a dead aim!")

8. If you have to play safe, *play safe!* This means that a player should take whatever club is required to get the ball into position for the next shot, away from any trouble.

I still have no problem with any of the above instructions.

But, disastrously, he also taught me two other things that ruined all the good advice that he gave me. Being told to "concentrate on the execution of the shot and not the result" was a mistake because it made me concentrate on my technique too much instead of just playing the game

and allowing matters to flow naturally. In the heat of competition one should only be concerned with rhythm and
target and forget about execution. I now try to play the game
as reactively as possible, visualizing and imagining the ball's
flight and nothing else. I do not find it an easy thing to do.

The most damaging advice of all, however, was the shut-
face takeaway. It undermined my most fervent hopes and
ambitions. I honed it to perfection in that little wooden
shed. A shut clubface at the transition from backswing to
downswing attack meant I had to "fan" the club open at
impact. I could never allow myself to release the club full
throttle. I was such a good athlete and my timing was so good
that I got away with it for years. None of the professionals
that I went to for instruction ever addressed this fatal flaw.

I am certain that the same flaw has been responsible for
Seve Ballesteros's demise as a competitive golfer. If only he
could find a way to neutralise the clubface throughout the
swing, he would rediscover his game and confidence.

The shut face concept that John drilled into me was a
misconception and a legacy of playing with whippy hickory
shafts. Ironically, I doubt very much if he actually played
that way himself. His wish to pass it on to me may have
been the product of the popular but infamous "square
method" which was "flavour of the decade" during the 1960s.
John must have read about this terrible heresy and erroneously
believed in it. The "square method" looked and sounded
good on paper but it ruined many a promising golfer.

I loved John's company and learned more about golf
from him than anyone else. Addressing the ball with my
back practically touching the wall of that little hut gave the
phrase "grooving the swing" real meaning. It certainly eliminated any possibility of "laying off" at the top. Within a
few weeks of John's death in 1974 I won my first major competition, the Castletroy Scratch Cup, which could be
classed as the Limerick City Open Championship. It
attracted all the top players from around the country. It was
a much bigger affair at the time than it is now, a fact that

can be confirmed by the names of the players who won it prior to me. After I won, it started to go downhill! I often wonder if John's car had loomed into view with a few holes to go on that memorable day, would the pressure of those eagle eyes watching have been too much and another dramatic collapse taken place?

⊗

CHAPTER 15

Local Heroes
Friends and Foes

I have played with many fine golfers over the years, and some of them made an indelible impression upon me.

Joseph B. Carr—The Sultan of Sutton

Joe Carr dominated Irish amateur golf like a colossus, as forty championship victories will testify. In the middle of his career he completely changed his swing and then changed it back again without it affecting his success rate. He began with a flat, scything, right-side-dominated action that featured a truncated follow-through as he drove the ball forward with his shoulder—à la Walter Hagen. In the mid-1960s, under the guidance of John Jacobs, he changed to a more orthodox, longer, and more upright swing before reverting back to his original, natural action. Joe was very long and wild off the tee but his recovery play was exceptional. He could get up and down in two shots from anywhere. I was but one of many who found themselves on the receiving end of his Houdini-like qualities. "If you can hit it, you can hole it" was his philosophy. His ability to pull off masterstrokes when he was in trouble was uncanny. Most of all, he played with an arrogant swagger that I envied.

Joe had fascinating hands. They were as big as shovels

Just when I thought I had Joe Carr beaten at the Irish Close Championship of 1967, it was me who got beaten on the last hole.

and seemed to cover the whole handle of the club. His right index finger was allowed to dangle like Billy the Kid about to pull the trigger. That is a good analogy because he was a cold-blooded killer in golfing terms. Joe's talents were particularly suitable to match play because he could unnerve an opponent with a telling shot when it was least expected.

We met for the first time in the Irish Close at Lahinch in 1967. I was raw, but I could play. Right from the beginning of the match, in front of a huge gallery, I had Joe in trouble. All the way around I was ahead and outplaying him. After fourteen holes I was two up and it probably would have been four if I had taken my chances. At the tenth, I left a ten-footer for a winning birdie "in the jaws" but short. Joe nonchalantly flicked my ball away with the disparaging comment, "Never up, never in." Then at the fifteenth, one of the hardest holes on the course, Joe holed a 45-footer for a birdie. That changed the match completely. One up is no lead. I followed Joe onto the dance floor at the par-three sixteenth but three-putted from fifteen yards, as nerves and excitement overcame me. Joe then said something that completely unhinged me, "I have been in this position thousands of times, you know."

The par-four seventeenth was out of reach in two, but Joe hit a magnificent driver off the deck onto the apron of the green. I hooked my second shot well left of the green into deep rough, but played a miraculous recovery to within a few feet of the hole. Unfazed, seen-it-all-before Joe took out his putter and holed from about a mile away. Now I was one down with one to go. At eighteen, Joe played two excellent wood shots and a gorgeous pitch to within a few inches of the hole to put me out of a championship that he went on to win in some style. However, in a local context, at least, my name as a golfer had been made. I asked Joe afterward for a few tips to help me improve my game but he only laughed at me and brushed me aside. Later, I complained bitterly to my guru, the great John Burke, about Joe's indifference and on-course comments. John only laughed and said I should have had the wit to answer him back with interest. He would only respect me if I stood up to him and beat the hell out of him.

What I did not know at the time, and John did not enlighten me, was that a youthful Carr had himself been the victim of similar gamesmanship from Burke in the 1946 "South" final. Apparently, Joe was outfoxed and intimidated more than he was outplayed by the so-called "King of Lahinch" enjoying his last hurrah. From that day on I have always made sure that if anybody said anything to me in the middle of a match that I did not like, they received a strong reaction.

Carr's greatest triumph was beating the reigning champion, Harvie Ward, in the final of the British Amateur at Hoylake in 1953. Ward was regarded as "unbeatable" at the time and easily the best amateur in the world. But Joe raised his game to a high level on the final nine holes. He also proved it was no fluke by winning "the Amateur" two more times.

Dr. David Sheahan—The Walking Pencil

David was an ungainly, awkward but effective player, who was able to hit the ball a long way using a very weak grip, a pigeon-toed stance, and a "flying" right elbow that caused him to cross the line alarmingly at the top of the swing. Those are but a few of his swing characteristics. But boy, was he unflappable and could he play! Nobody wins three Irish Close Championships by just being lucky. He used a very heavy blade putter that I reckon was bought for 7s. 6d. (old money), equivalent to $1, at Clery's Department Store. It sank an awful lot of putts in its day, thanks to an unusual method. With hands well behind the ball at address, he made a forward press that got everything into position at the last moment and bang she went down the hatch.

His medical profession meant that he was a true-blue amateur, and that he could only play a very limited schedule of events. Yet he was a factor nearly every time he showed up throughout the 1960s and 1970s. One of my proudest days was in April of 1974 when I managed to beat him in a

The winning putt at the Castletroy Scratch Cup of 1974.

My victory in the '74 Castletroy Cup was the first of three.

tight finish to win the Castletroy Scratch Cup for the first
of three times that I won that prestigious event. (It is one
of the top 36-hole competitions in Irish golf.) After I had
muffed a shot at the twelfth in the afternoon round, I overheard one of my supporters and mentors, the late Dr. John
Angelo Holmes, say to somebody, "That's it. Sheahan will
win it now. He is the class player in the tournament, anyway."

At Castletroy, John's remark did not please me at all. In
fact it made me mad as hell, similar to the way Bob Drum
got Arnold Palmer going at the U.S. Open at Cherry Hills
in 1960, and I managed to recover and finish strong to
shoot an afternoon 69 to go with my morning 71. To beat
Sheahan was a special thrill. He was indeed a class act and
proved it beyond all doubt when he conquered a field of
top professionals at Royal Dublin in 1962 to win the Jeyes
Tournament, the last time an amateur has won on the
European Tour.

Sheahan also had the distinction of defeating the British Amateur Champion Ron Davies and U.S. Amateur Champion Labron Harris Jr. on successive days during the 1963 Walker Cup matches. Never before, or since, did a seven-and-six-penny putter achieve so much.

Jackie Harrington—Mr. Super Cool

Without Jackie Harrington in the ranks, it is doubtful that Limerick Golf Club would have won the Irish Senior Cup in 1976 and 1980, or the European Clubs' Cup in 1980. He put a touch of titanium into the team. When the European Cup was slipping from our grasp it was Jackie who somehow rallied and found a way to make a fantastic birdie at the tough eighteenth at Santa Ponza that gained us that lousy, mangy, miserable one-shot winning margin. I will never forget that, nor will I forget the drama that took place earlier that day. Jackie accidentally locked himself into his room the night before. He did not respond to his wake-up call and did not show up for breakfast. Our telephone calls

Official presentation at the 1980 European Team Championship. Left to right: Jackie Harrington, Pat Cotter (nonplaying captain), the author, Vincent Nevin.

to his room went unanswered. Time was ticking away. The master key could not be found. Our team's Captain, Pat Cotter, was growing more frantic by the minute. Even though Jackie's room was eight stories up in a Spanish high-rise, there was only one thing to do: I put aside my fear of heights and climbed from one balcony to the next and entered Jackie's room via the sliding door. I dragged him out of bed and (still in his pyjamas) pushed him under the shower. He told me later he did not recover from this treatment until he reached the final hole and that if I had not been so rough on him he would have found his composure sooner and none of us would have had to sweat so much.

Jackie Harrington was a brilliant boy golfer at Adare, winning the Munster Boys' Championship in 1952 and 1953. He plays exactly the same way fifty years later. Strong grip. Wide stance. Big shoulder turn. Wonderful hand action. Unflappable temperament. His aggressive and fearless attitude toward the game was always a joy for me to play beside in alternate shot format. My jarring, nervous game steadied up considerably thanks to my exposure to Jackie. He could not care less if you ran every putt six feet past the hole. That suited me fine. Our gung-ho attitude paid off in the Barton Shield Final at Tramore in 1976. We began our morning round with five birdies. With his encouragement, we went for everything. It was a fantastic feeling. Jackie told me, "Never be short with your first couple of putts. Show the opposition that you are not afraid and mean business."

Jackie's only weakness was that he did not have a clue how to club himself. When he saw me pacing off courses and taking notes, he thought it was hilarious and teased me about it. Soon enough, though, he was knocking on my door looking for a copy of my hard work. To teach him a lesson, I once gave him a cockeyed set of measurements. But it took him longer than it should have to find out he had been tricked.

Jackie has the unique distinction of being an Irish Close Champion and an Irish Senior Champion. His prowess as a golfer has receded very little over the years. He plays a simple game and does not bother much with technical claptrap. The game comes easily to him.

Vincent Nevin—The Pocket Battleship
When Vincent Nevin joined Limerick Golf Club in 1966, a golden era of achievement for the club began. Between 1966 and 1973, Vincent never lost a match for the club. His dedicated and thoughtful approach was inspiring and a great headline to follow. The rest of us raised our games in support and together we went on the warpath.

Vincent was self-taught. Ever since his caddieing days at Ennis, he built his game around a very strong grip that no teaching professional would have countenanced. He had two distinct swings, one for wooden play and another for iron play. But he was a master of both. On the other hand, most of the time he had no putting game at all! Whenever Vincent putted well, he was unbeatable. With wooden clubs, a figure eight loop—which included banging the shaft off the back of his neck—achieved outstandingly consistent results. Although Vincent was small of stature, he was mega-long and straight. This gave him a mastery over par-five holes and reduced the par of every course he played by at least a couple of strokes. His compact, controlled swing with iron clubs rendered extremely accurate results. I found it puzzling that I could regularly use two clubs fewer on approach shots but could rarely outdrive him. He had his very own way of playing and he stuck with it. The only time he seemed to care about what the opposition was doing was on the putting green. In this area, his negativity was laughable. When I had to partner him in alternate shot format, he drove me mad by begging me to lag the shortest of putts when I saw no reason not to try to hole everything in sight.

Vincent retired prematurely after we won the European Cup in 1980. The pressure of having to hole those short putts was getting to him. It is a pity the young members do not have the opportunity to watch Vincent prepare for an upcoming tournament. He concentrated on hitting hundreds of balls every evening, rather than playing a casual game. He always played to a plan, analysing the next tournament venue and working assiduously at whatever particular shots he thought would be needed to play it successfully.

James "Jazz" Carew—Tail Gunner Supreme

"On the tee, please, representing Limerick Golf Club, James Carew."

"Mr. Menton, I am not hitting before my time."

"Mr. Carew, I am tired of standing here in the cold. Please drive off."

"No way. I am here to win the Irish Junior Cup, not for your convenience."

It was another one of those biblical David and Goliath encounters. Bill Menton, the long-serving Ayatollah of Irish golf, pined for the sanctuary of a warm clubhouse. But our

The author and James Carew.

James was not budging. Those who were there and those who know Mr. Menton were astonished that somebody as small and frail as James, playing in his first Irish final, would talk to the feared General Secretary of the Golfing Union of Ireland in such a manner. If the members of the U.S. PGA Tour thought Dean Beman was hard to take sometimes, they certainly would not have liked dealing with Bill Menton, the efficient but dictatorial ruler of Irish amateur golf for many years. My pal James had been selected to represent Limerick in the critical Number Five (tail gunner) position in the delayed Irish Junior Cup Final of 1975 at Royal Portrush. And that was the place in which he was going to stay and play—no matter how cold Bill Menton was! James was keenly aware that the tactics involved in naming the order in which a team went out to play could mean the difference between winning and losing. Menton knew too, but he did not care.

Quickly sizing up the situation, I did my duty. I grabbed James by the arm and led him away and told him to go around to the back of the pro shop until I called him. The reason for the hubbub was because our fourth player, Raymond Smyth, had inconveniently lost his opening drive and was returning to the teeing ground to reload. If James had driven off, he would have been out of his nominated position, and our carefully thought-out tactics would have been rendered obsolete. James won the battle of wills, and Limerick did win the Irish Junior Cup for the first time ever. Subsequently, James went on to be part of four Irish Junior Cup winning teams, a feat that nobody else in the hundred-year history of the competition has equalled.

Apart from the day my father died, the greatest sense of loss I ever experienced was when my favourite golf partner, confidante, and soul mate, James Carew, died completely unexpectedly on June 29th, 1998. We had been pals since our schooldays. We were a formidable team both on and off the golf course, pooling our ideas to find ways of improving our own play and the success rate of Limerick Golf Club teams. A lack of natural strength and body weight put up barriers to James getting to the top of sports (he never showed any interest in being a jockey!), but he was highly talented and skilled at any game involving a ball. He had one of the most astute sports brains I ever came across. He really understood the "psychology" of competitive sport. Pound for pound he was a truly great player. On a fast-running course, he could scald far stronger hitters. His cool head and ability under pressure were legendary. Being a traditionalist, he turned up his nose at metal woods when they arrived on the scene. I pleaded with him to reequip himself and take advantage of the priceless extra length they would bring to his game. He resisted, but eventually capitulated. His handicap immediately dropped to two and he won an Irish Senior cup medal to go with his four junior medals, a unique achievement.

We were a bit of a dream team together on committees, always working in tandem. I would go in with all guns blazing and then James would follow up with a compromise. This often won the day and we would both go home happy. In a crisis James had the ability to remain composed, whereas I would become emotional and lose my head.

"It is not what you say, but the way that you say it that gets you into trouble," he counselled. He was right, of course. James knew better than I did how to get his point across without offending. But, as Bill Menton found out, he was no shrinking violet either. And he could cut you up in pieces with a remark if he felt you deserved it.

James had a countrywide reputation for being a scrupulously fair, generous but hard-as-nails opponent, and he was respected all over Ireland. What more can I say except I miss him a lot more than I could ever have imagined possible. He is also missed by his other golfing pals at Ballyclough and Lahinch. He would, I am sure, want us to play on, in his own outstanding tradition.

*Limerick Golf Club Centenary Competition Organizing Committee
(1991). Left to right: Jack Lynch, Billy Rice, Terry Clancy, the author.*

Billy Rice—The Boy Blunder

"I am not hitting another shaggin' ball," I shouted, "until
you put it on the fairway!"

I had lost the cool once more. This time it was while playing for Munster in the 1976 Inter-provincial Championship
at Carlow, one of Ireland's few true heathland courses.

My partner Billy Rice and I were the best of friends,
roommates, and travelling companions. But on the golf
course, playing the same ball in an alternate shot match,
our games were not compatible.

Our opponents, Bob Pollin and Brian Kissock of Ulster,
must have wondered what the hell was going on. Here was
that mad Ivan blowing a fuse again and giving them the
match on a plate. Like hell, I was!

Billy and I had lost three out of the first four holes. This
was because in each case my partner had put our ball under
a tree and I had no way of hitting for the green. Going to the
fifth tee I issued a stern warning: "Find the fairway, or else!"

So what does Billy do? At No. 5, he aims his tee shot down the line of trees on the right-hand side of this long hole, hoping to draw it back into prime position. The shot never turned, and straight-as-a-die it flew into yet another tree. So I marched down to the ball, picked it up and threw it at him. Naturally he was shocked, and so was everybody else in the vicinity. Now we were four down on the sixth tee and in no-man's-land. We needed to produce fireworks or be slaughtered like innocents. In my anger I found the zone. I hit a four-iron to the par-three sixth stone dead. Billy, seething inside, and definitely not talking to me because of my insulting behaviour, creamed a beauty up the middle of the seventh fairway.

"A fairway at last," I said sarcastically.

Another fine approach set up another birdie. Then another and another and another followed. Ulster were overtaken and destroyed. Coming off the final green all was sweetness and light between my partner and me again, and both of us were looking forward to playing a more conventional and less stressful game in the afternoon.

Unfortunately, our team captain, Bob Fluery, was not at all pleased. He disciplined me and dropped me from the starting lineup and left Billy in my place. I got no credit for my successful psychology. By winning, I thought I had proved my point and would be forgiven.

Despite several similar incidents between us, I have nothing but the highest regard and gratitude toward Billy Rice. I could not have had a better companion with whom to travel around the country, going to all of the tournaments we played in together. He was a vital part of the successful Limerick teams we played on. I always had full confidence in his ability to be able to beat anybody on a particular day. Like myself, he could snatch defeat from the jaws of victory on occasion. That is where his nickname, "The Boy Blunder," came from. Team captains knew in advance that both of us were well capable of "blowing" a match, but rarely did the two of us do it at the same time. When both

of us won—which occurred more often than not—
Limerick Golf Club was as good as "home and dry."

Rupert De Lacy "Wellington" Staunton

It is a major miscarriage of justice that such an enormously
talented golfer as Rupert Staunton did not win a Walker
Cup cap. He regularly reached the final stages of the Irish
Close and British Amateur and always gave a good account
of himself at the International level when playing for
Ireland. In 1967 he was selected to play in the Walker Cup
trials but was deprived of an automatic place on the team
when Major Ronnie Blair pulled out due to illness with only
his match with Rupert remaining to be played. At the time,
nobody thought it made any difference because Rupert was
well ahead of Blair in the Round Robin ranking points. But
the selectors stunned all of Ireland by selecting Blair and
ignoring Staunton. My guess is that the ever casual Rupert
must have upset the selectors by turning up to play in his
Wellington boots, as he was reported to have done many
times at home in Castlerea. This habit can be explained by
his self-appointed position of part-time greenkeeper at his
home club. If Rupert did not cut the greens it would not
have been done often enough—or perhaps not at all.
Sometimes he was talked off his tractor and obliged "to
make up a four" by his fellow members. By all accounts, his
not bothering to change his footwear did not affect his
standard of play one little bit.

I managed to preserve an unbeaten record against
Rupert in three championship matches but I was fortunate
to do so, as can be illustrated by the story of one of our bat-
tles. We were drawn to play each other in the first round of
the Irish Close at Royal Dublin in 1986. After destroying
par on the first nine, I was five up. On the tenth tee, Rupert
told me he was on the point of retiring to become a selector and this was going to be his last match in championship
golf. If he thought I would fall for this bit of blarney and
slacken my grip, he was wrong. Besides, selectors were not

my favourite people. I continued to play steadily, and eventually I stood five up with five holes to play. At the fourteenth, Rupert was on the edge of the green and I was well inside him. Casually, and without hardly looking at what he was doing, he holed out. He was mildly displeased because he now had to turn away from the clubhouse and head back out into the country again. At the fifteenth, I drove into a divot and could not extricate myself well enough and lost the hole. No. 16 at Royal Dublin is a short, driveable par four in favourable conditions. Rupert sliced short and to the right. I hit a good one onto the apron of the green. Rupert pitched to about ten feet. I putted up to three feet. He holed and I missed. I hit two good shots at No. 17 to about twenty feet; Rupert was thirty feet away. You guessed it: He holed and I missed. Panic stations! Down the famous garden hole we went. Two perfect drives. Rupert hit his second shot just short of the par-five green about sixty feet away. I was thirty yards short but played a good approach to three feet and felt sure it must be over now. Without breaking stride, Rupert gave his ball a careless belt. The ball sped forward and clattered against the flag before slowly squeezing itself below ground. I could have been shot! I was stunned, but said nothing, picked up my ball marker and, head down, strode toward the nineteenth tee. I was there for a couple of minutes trying to compose myself and anxiously waiting for another match to clear the fairway, when I noticed Rupert was missing. I looked back toward the green and saw him talking to a gaggle of reporters. He saw me glaring at him and he beckoned me. Reluctantly I walked over, whereupon he thrust his hand forward and said, "I am not playing anymore. I have retired. Best of luck to you for the rest of the week. Let's go and have a pint!" The newspapers made a feast of the story the next day.

It must have been a week for incidents, because while practicing for the same championship a few days earlier I played what has to be one of the most unusual shots ever. It was at the garden hole, No. 18 at Royal Dublin. This hole is a sharp dogleg to the right at which, if the green is to be reached in two shots, one has to aim across the large practice area and overcome a long, intimidating carry of two hundred yards or more. Anything short or right of this carry is out of bounds. Playing with Royal Dublin member Gerry O'Donovan and my Limerick Golf Club friend Michael Galvin for a few punts, I hit my drive into perfect position. Gerry's ball was about four or five feet past mine, directly in line with the flag. I decided to use his ball as a guide to line up my shot in the gathering dusky gloom. The strike felt fine but there was a loud click as my ball caromed off the ball lying in front. We all saw one of the balls bounding across the practice ground (it turned out to be Gerry's), but nobody saw where my ball went. I reloaded and played an awful effort to the right and out of bounds. Gerry saw some Limerick money coming to him so he played safely up beyond the turn in the fairway and then pitched onto the green in three. When we arrived at the green, there was a ball with a large black burn mark on the cover lying one foot from the hole. It was my original ball. Some fellows watching from behind the green said they heard a noise and wondered what it was. They were further mystified by the manner in which my ball had alighted on the green, and wondered who was able to play such a shot.

One said, "It seemed to drop straight out of the sky."

Pat Ruddy — Dreamer and Course Builder

"We make no apology that the thoughtless or inept player may suffer on our links," is the uncompromising philosophy of Pat Ruddy, owner of The European Club at Brittas Bay, thirty miles south of Dublin. Yet, there is a fulsome welcome and friendly disposition toward visiting players at one of the world's youngest and greatest links courses.

Links golf is very rare in the context of world golf. There are only about 150 links courses in the entire world and almost a third of them can be found in Ireland. The type of dunesland needed is finite and little is available, in Ireland or anywhere else. So imagine what it must feel like to own such a unique facility, having conceived the idea, found the land, and built the course all by yourself. Having the courage, dedication, and skill to develop a golf course out of nothing with restricted financial resources is an incredible feat. Against the odds and despite the skeptics, it was achieved by Pat Ruddy.

Amongst golfing dreamers, most speculate about winning championships. Ruddy dreamt of building a links course that would reflect his fundamentalist attitude toward golf architecture. He achieved his dream quite brilliantly. The European Club (I do not particularly care for that name myself, and have argued with Ruddy that he should at least add the word "Golfers" to it) can stand shoulder-to-shoulder with any of the world's great courses—links or otherwise—in my opinion.

If Pat were not so proud of his desire "to do it all by himself" and allowed outside investors to put money into the project, he would be closer to the possibility of getting it into the ultimate shape and to the possibility that a top class professional tournament would take place at his facility. That would deservedly make it a lot more famous than it already is. He does not care. His independence of thought and action makes him worthy of being one of golf's greatest little known heroes—and his golf course is of a similar mold.

❦

CHAPTER 16

The Irish and the U.S. Open

The first American-bred player to win the U.S. Open was Johnny McDermott in 1911. But with a name like that, he had to be Irish! One of the players he beat in a playoff was another "Irishman," Mike Brady. When McDermott won again the following year, Tom McNamara, who had family connections with Lahinch, was runner-up and Mike Brady was third. Now there is a good trivia question: In what year did three Irishmen fill the first three places in a major? McDermott was actually born in Philadelphia in 1891 (the year Limerick GC was founded) to Irish-born parents. He came to golf the best way, through caddieing.

In the opinion of experts of that period, the best player never to win the U.S. Open was Mike Brady. He was also the son of Irish-born parents who had immigrated to Boston. Mike had as many unsuccessful chances to win the U.S. Open as Sam Snead. In 1914, he was fifth. In 1915, sixth. In 1916, ninth. In 1919, he tied Walter Hagen for first place but was beaten in the playoff. In 1925, he was seventh. If you look up the records of early U.S. Opens, you will see names like J.J. O'Brien, Tom Boyd, Tom and George Kerrigan, Willie Maguire, Eugene McCarthy, Pat Doyle, Tom Mulgrew, John Shea, Johnny Farrell, Frank and Tom Walsh, and Pat and Peter O'Hara. The O'Hara's had an older brother, Jimmy, who won the Irish Professional Championship in 1914. Pat O'Hara also won "the Irish" in 1919 before emmigrating to America to join his brother Peter, who was already Head Professional at the Richmond Club on Staten Island. Three years later Pat won the famous North and South Open at Pinehurst, beating a field that included Gene Sarazen, Jock Hutchinson, and Walter Hagen. Later in 1922, Pat was tied 35th behind winner Gene Sarazen in the U.S. Open at Skokie CC. Mike Brady was eighth. Pat grew homesick and went back to Ireland, never to return to America. He retained his golf skills because he won the Irish Professional Championship again in 1927. One can only surmise what he might have achieved if he had remained in America, or if transatlantic travel was more accessible in those days. Peter O'Hara, not to be outdone by his brothers, tied for seventh in the 1924 U.S. Open at Oakland Hills, and until 2000 it remained the highest finish by a natural-born Irishman in the championship. This is without doubt the "golden era" of the Irish in the U.S. Open. Nowadays, even with easy travel, we are lucky to have anybody playing in it. Perhaps the best chance of an Irishman winning the U.S. Open may already be long gone, not withstanding Padraig Harrington's creditable performance in finishing a distant fifth to Tiger at Pebble Beach in 2000.

⊛

CHAPTER 17

Three Florida Crackers and a Nut

Dr. David Kern Davis
"I would like to know how the greatest golf nut in America met up with the greatest golf nut in Ireland," the lady said. Without missing a beat or looking up from my newspaper, I replied, "It was inevitable."

This exchange took place in Fran Davis's kitchen in St. Petersburg, Florida. Fran is the wife of one of the most impressive people I have met throughout my golf-saturated life: Dr. David Kern Davis. It was hardly inevitable, as I had claimed, but it certainly makes you wonder about the power of fate.

The Davis family lives beside the golf course in St. Petersburg that I played as a student while attending nearby Eckerd College. I was there on an International Students Fellowship Scholarship in 1965–1966 sponsored by the Rotary Club of Tampa. Strangely, we never met during my time as a student, even though I played the golf course, Lakewood, regularly. Dave and I also attended the same church on Sundays without our paths ever crossing. I cycled past his house many times, which looks out onto the sixteenth fairway, and we must surely have hit balls side-by-side on the practice ground because both of us spent a lot of time there. Somehow we never met, which is almost as strange as how we did meet, years later, quite accidentally.

Dr. David Davis at the controls.

On a bright, sunny evening at Lahinch in July of 1983, I was playing on my own to prepare for the upcoming South of Ireland Championship. Approaching the fourteenth green, I noticed a flashing green glow on the tenth tee nearby. My curiosity was aroused. I called across to the group on the tenth, "What sort of a club is that? It is glowing green!" One word returned another and I walked up to the tee. One of the group, Dr. Joe Burns, was waggling his titanium-shafted prototype driver and the sun's rays were glancing off of it. "This is space age technology," he said, "and it's going to have a big impact on golf club manufacturing in the future." Fascinated, I asked if I could I hit a shot with this strange-looking club. Aiming down the tenth fairway, I launched one about as well as I ever have. I thanked Joe for allowing me to hit the shot with his club, but before I turned to walk away I casually asked them where they were from.

"Florida"

"I know Florida well. I went to college there. What part of Florida?"

"A city called St. Petersburg."

"Wow!" I said. "That's where I was. At Eckerd College. I played my golf at Lakewood."

"We're members of Lakewood!"

"Is Skip Alexander still going strong?"

"Do you know Skip?"

The conversation went on in this vein as the amazing coincidence began to sink in. I said I would finish my round and wait for them to do likewise and we would have a longer chat. Dave Davis was part of the group, and later that evening when he heard I was a member at Ballybunion he asked me if I would take him there for a game on the brand new Cashen Course. That was easily arranged and a great friendship began. Dave has come to Ireland practically every year since, and by now knows parts of Ireland better than I do.

Dave grew up in Old Greenwich, Connecticut, but during his high school years he lived right beside Merion Golf Club in Ardmore, Pennsylvania. His father was a childhood friend of Jerome Kern, who wrote the famous musicals. Dave never met Kern personally, but he carries his name. It is slightly intriguing for both of us that the name of my family's printing company is McKern, but where that name came from is quite another story.

Dave went to Fordham University in New York, enlisted in the Army, and finished his medical studies at Georgetown University in Washington, D.C. He interned at Gorgas in the Panama Canal Zone, where he became a bit of an expert on tropical diseases. Following several years of general practice in Harlan County in Kentucky, he finished Pathology training and settled in St. Petersburg, Florida in 1954. There he was baptised in Nuclear Medicine and years later helped to introduce nuclear magnetic resonance to the west coast of Florida. He told me himself that he always resented the dropping of "Nuclear" from NMR. I told him that it was probably because it was a word that makes a lot of people nervous.

When he moved to Florida, he quickly saw the need for an air ambulance business to transport the deceased who had passed away in the Tampa Bay region back up North for burial in their home cities. After ten years in business with a small group of other pilots, fuel prices went through the roof so he bought and converted a Greyhound bus to replace the twin-engine plane that he'd used. On weekends during the fall, the bus doubled as a great transportation/party machine for University of Florida football games all over the Southeast. An additional job was to use his Piper Cub to take photographs from the air, primarily property for real estate appraisers. Even after thirty years, Dave still does this work with some relish and a broad smile on his face. I know because I have been up there with him. In the process he has photographed almost every inch of the Tampa Bay region from the air.

Since his student days Dave has been a scratch golfer, regularly playing in the top amateur and professional tournaments around Florida. At one stage of his golfing life, he carried out an unusual experiment. Having reached scratch handicap right-handed, he thought he might be able to play better from the other side because he is left-handed in all activities off the golf course. It was not a total failure because he reached a single-digit handicap fairly rapidly before his patience ran out and he reverted to playing right-handed again.

Dave has told me many wonderful stories about his golfing adventures. Here is one of my personal favourites:

Back in the sixties, a group of hotshot players from the Tampa Bay area regularly travelled together to the big tournaments in the Southeast. Jimmy Mann, the well-known and delightful golf columnist with the *St. Petersburg Times*, often accompanied them and sometimes shared a room with Dave. Jimmy was held in some awe by his peers, so he shamelessly used his position to make life easier. Back in those pre-Internet days, filing copy by telegraph was a time-consuming and tedious business. Whenever he could, Mann employed a young trainee from the local newspaper to do the hard graft.

On one occasion, Mann became aware that his young assistant was "borrowing" his copy and running it almost verbatim in the local rag. After returning from playing the final round of the tourney, Dave found his roommate's latest opus in the typewriter almost complete. He could not resist reading it. It was a colourful piece about a noisy frog who sat in the lily pond beside the twelfth tee all day, seemingly heckling the hapless, sensitive golfers by croaking "Ribbit!" at them before they swung. He went on to say that quite a few were unnerved and performed accordingly by hitting their tee shots straight into the pond. When Jimmy returned to the room, Dave questioned him about this piece of fiction.

"Where did you get this blarney from, Jimmy? That story could not be true. There isn't a lily pond anywhere on the golf course!"

Jimmy explained how his copy was being purloined and that he had to do something to protect himself and teach the young man a lesson. "I have already sent in my report," he chortled. "This one is for 'Junior!'"

"How do you ever think of such things, Jimmy?"

"I guess it is what got me an 'A' in English," replied Mann.

My friend Dr. Davis is fascinated by Ireland. He understands its history, economics, and society. A lot of his knowledge is due to his mother, who was born in Ireland, and also to the books and press material that I have sent him. When he retired from medicine in 1993, he accepted an appointment as Chairman of the United Bank of Florida and led its flotation onto the Stock Exchange. For a year or two during a teacher shortage crisis, Dave helped out by teaching physics at the local high school. He is also a fine landscape and portrait painter and can play the piano. You would be forgiven if you thought there was no end to the man's talents. But there is: He cannot putt!

Dave and I have been embroiled in many escapades since we became partners in golf travels around Ireland and in Florida. One concerns a pair of alligator shoes. One day at Ballybunion I met and played golf with an American visitor named Rich Saurhaft. He was an executive with *Golf Illustrated* magazine at the time, so we had a common interest. After the round, I invited Rich to my home, and I took him to Lahinch the following day. He told me he was in a position to purchase golf gear at factory discount prices, and asked me if there was anything he could send from America that I could not get in Ireland. After some thought, I asked him to purchase a particular pair of Foot-Joy alligator shoes and gave him the necessary funds. My instructions were that he should send them to Dr. Davis in St. Pete because he was due to come to Ireland soon. Rich carried out my wishes in exemplary fashion. On the other hand, Davis did not pay proper attention to my taped message telling him to expect the shoes. When the shoes arrived, he thought they were a forgotten prize that he had won in some outing. So he began wearing them.

Late one evening, Dave was playing a few holes at Lakewood after working at the airport all day. He was enjoying the bright blue golf cart that had just been presented to him as a retirement gift by his colleagues at St. Anthony's Hospital, and he was wearing my shoes. A pushed tee shot at the thirteenth hole went into the pond that borders the fairway. While trying to recover the ball he did not notice that the cart had slipped its brake and was slowly rolling toward the water. In she went for a bath, with Dave too late to avert disaster. As his lovely new cart sank in the mud, Dave had to move quickly to save his clubs and anything else of value. The new shoes were destroyed as he sank up to his knees in swampy gunge. Eventually the course maintenance crew had to use lifting equipment to pull the cart back to dry land. After a thorough washing and greasing, the cart was no worse for its adventure—but not so the shoes. Dave left them beside the back door of his house to dry out under the hot Florida sun. The next morning the shoes were dry all right, but they had been chewed to bits by a low class hungry rodent overnight! That was but a minor disappointment and inconvenience until Dave arrived in Limerick and was promptly asked about the whereabouts of my alligator shoes. The look of horror on his face was something to behold as it dawned on him that the eaten shoes were mine. All we could do was laugh and hope that the "dirty rat" that had eaten my lovely shoes had choked.

George (Mr. Two-Bits) Edmondson Jr.
"Two bits, four bits, six bits, a dollar. All for the Gators, stand up and holler!"

It may sound simple and even childish, but George Edmondson is a celebrity all over Florida because of his football cheers. He can barely take a step outdoors without being greeted by someone or other wishing to discuss the progress of the University of Florida (Gators) team, and all because he has led his famous cheer during every game at Gainesville for fifty years. When the team was down on its luck and poorly supported, it was George who became the

"Mr. Two-Bits" (George Edmondson) does his stuff in "The Swamp" in Gainesville.

rallying point, and on his own rekindled the mute supporters' fervour. Almost single-handedly, he brought passion and a smile to UF football games, especially those played in Gainesville. A few quick shrills of his whistle and a wave of his paper baton would alert the fans to his whereabouts in the stand. With arms flailing and histrionics in full swing, "Mr. Two-Bits" could bring a stadium of 80,000 souls to its feet.

I have been blessed to have had two fathers. My natural Dad, Tom, of whom I was very fond, and also a "foster" father in Tampa, Florida: one George Edmondson Jr. I spent every weekend in Tampa with George and his family while I was a student at Eckerd College. He looked after me like a true son. We played golf at Palma Ceia CC and quite a few other courses in the area. It was a wonderful year—one of the best of my life—and I will be forever grateful.

On one of our visits to Tampa, Marie and I borrowed George's 1960s vintage Oldsmobile (which I used to call "the aircraft carrier" because it was so big) to go to Orlando. Throughout the journey, people waved and honked their greetings. We could not figure out why until it dawned on us that the car's license plate read "2-Bits." When we returned to Tampa, George told us that the police in Orlando had called him to say a "strange" couple was seen driving his car in central Florida. George reassured them all was in order so we did not suffer the embarrassment of being asked for identification and having to give an account of ourselves. Such is the esteem and fame of my Florida foster father, George "Two-Bits" Edmondson Jr.

Stewart "Skip" Alexander

Skip Alexander died in 1998 just short of his eightieth birthday. Anyone who knows his life history knows that it is a miracle he reached that age at all. This is because in September of 1950, while in third place on the U.S. PGA Tour money list, Skip was involved in a plane crash in which he was the only survivor of the four people on board. Seriously injured, he lay in a hospital bed for three months, suffering

The beautifully balanced swing of Stewart "Skip" Alexander, circa 1950.

from multiple fractures and severe burns. He then had to endure five further months of plastic surgery. His hands were particularly badly damaged. The extensors were all contracted so tightly that they did not have any openings. The surgeons separated them and opened them up. A plastic bar was inserted by taking a knuckle out of each finger. The remaining two knuckles were fused together so that Skip could hold a golf club. The doctors were ordered to do this by Skip himself, who insisted he would play golf again. After 75 operations in all, Skip did return to golf, and then performed a second miracle by winning a place on the 1951 U.S. Ryder Cup team. At the Ryder Cup Matches in Albany, New York, he played Scotland's John Panton. With his hands bandaged and bleeding, and unsure if he could walk

36 holes, Skip did what any sensible fellow would do in such circumstances—he won early, by 8/7.

Dave Davis swears Skip had it in him to be as good as Hogan and Snead until that cruel accident stopped him in his tracks. Having played with him a few times myself in the "Ten Dollar" game at Lakewood, when he was an old man, I could see that he could surely play golf, even if he was only barely able to shuffle from his golf cart to his ball because of his damaged legs. He loved his golf cart; it gave him back the ability to get around a golf course. Hitting the ball was the easy part; walking the golf course was another story. I smile when I think of the day we were going up the long sixth at Lakewood. As usual I was walking along quite briskly well ahead of the carts. Skip glided up beside me and said, "There he is, the mad Irishman, leaning into the golf course. That is the way they walk over there, because of the wind."

Skip's inability to walk a golf course day after day forced him into early retirement, but he continued to compete with great success at local one-day events around Florida and the Carolinas whenever he was allowed to use a cart. He loved to win. Never grew tired of it. When I was a student playing at Lakewood, he was very kind to me and always greeted me when I entered his shop with the words: "You wanna play, Irish? Off you go and make some birdies."

Skip was widely acknowledged as a great teacher. Jack Grout, Jack Nicklaus's instructor at Scioto Country Club in Ohio, sent Nicklaus to Skip when the Golden Bear was a youngster. It did not do Jack any harm that a lot of people noticed. Skip's son Buddy, who is currently head coach to the University of Florida golf team, won the U.S. Amateur in 1986. I very much regret that I did not take a proper series of lessons from Skip, instead of just making do with the odd tip here and there. His popularity at Lakewood was clearly evident, and he was made "Pro Emeritus in Perpetuity" when he retired from active duty in 1984. He continued to play golf with the members nearly every day for another fourteen years, showing an amazing passion and love for the game right up to the end of his painful but happy life.

Tom Jewell — Golf Nut Par Excellence

Fran Davis may think her husband is America's greatest golf nut, but she's wrong. That distinction belongs to Lavon Jewell's fella, and she has the certification to prove it. In 1997, Tommy Jewell was officially named "Golf Nut of the Year" by the Golf Nut Society of America. It was a richly deserved honour. I met Tom at Black Diamond Ranch in 1992. He joined our group at what was then Florida's most exciting new course. At the time Tom was Tournament Director of the JC Penney Classic, having just retired from a senior executive position with that company. He mesmerised me with his intimate, personal knowledge of every golfer, male or female, on the U.S. pro tours. I was in my element conversing with him. I found out one of Tom's hobbies was saving golf balls with logos. When I got home to

Tom Jewell, "1997 Golf Nut of the Year," at Florida's Black Diamond Ranch.

Ireland I set about saving balls with exclusively Irish logos on them and sent them to him. That started an exchange of golf books, anecdotes, and ideas across the ocean that carries on to this day.

The citation that declared Tom "Golf Nut of the Year" includes such gems as:

- Played golf on first day of honeymoon. There was snow on the ground. It was a balmy 31 f. degrees. New Bride, Lavon, walked the course with him but did not play. They are still together 43 years later, but now she does play.
- In 1985, he hurt his back and was told to stay in bed for three weeks. During the first week, a friend called with an invitation to play Augusta National. Tom phoned his doctor and was told not to even think about it. Tom lay still for 10 days and then went to Augusta on his 55th birthday and played.
- For the past fifteen years, on the Monday morning after each event, he has written a personal note of congratulation to every winner on the PGA, LPGA, and Senior Tours. He has also written to every major award winner in golf congratulating them on their special recognition. Those from whom he has received replies include Ben Hogan, Byron Nelson, Ben Crenshaw, Jack Nicklaus, Arnold Palmer, Tom Watson, Sam Snead, Dave Marr, Patty Berg, Phil Mickelson, Raymond Floyd, Deane Beman, Pat Bradley, Hale Irwin, and Tom Kite. This collection is well worth seeing in his special golf den in his home.

Over the years, Tom collected over 6,000 individually logoed golf balls. When moving to a new house a few years ago, they became a bit of a problem to transport so he donated them to the Chi Chi Rodriguez Junior Golf Program. He still has 500 balls, including Presidential balls from Nixon, Ford, Reagan, and Bush. (President Clinton scattered so many balls around the links at Ballybunion during a visit in 1998 that I am amazed I was unable to find one to add to Tom's collection. By the way, the local people of Ballybunion were so delighted with this particular golfing president's visit, they built a seven-foot-high statue of the man in golfing pose at the eastern entrance to the town.

Tom Jewell has played 42 of the world's top hundred rated courses. Augusta National, 6 times. Pine Valley, 20 times. Shinnecock Hills, 15 times. Pinehurst #2, 12 times. Merion, 8 times. St. Andrews, twice. He has served on the Board of Directors of American Golf Sponsors, which is a group representing the sponsors of PGA Tour events. He holds a certificate in Professional Golf Instruction and has played golf with over 150 LPGA and PGA Tour Professionals during the past twenty years and regularly shoots his age in the 300 or more rounds of golf he plays annually.

It is obvious that Tom loves the game, so I was correct when I said to Fran Davis that it was inevitable that the biggest golf nut in Ireland should meet up with, and become firm friends with, his counterpart in America.

⊛

CHAPTER 18

The Search for the Perfect Swing
By an impure golfer

For far too long in my golf career, I was as famous for being a club thrower and a thrower of fits as I was for being a contender. This always caused me extreme embarrassment and remorse afterward. But it was too late. The damage had been done. In middle age, I am not really consoled by the realization that I did not do any harm to anyone but myself, and my prospects of achieving the highest honours in the game. Finally, and irrevocably, I learned my lesson when playing at Lakewood one day with Dave Davis. For the last time, but certainly not for the first time, my putter quite inexplicably found itself marooned up a tree. No matter how we tried we could not dislodge it or shake it loose. It was there to stay. Eventually, Dave got the bright idea to go home for his air gun, saying he would "shoot the S.O.B. out of the tree!" There we were, in the middle of doing just that, when a police patrol car came around the corner.

"Hey! What are you guys doing?"

"We are trying to shoot my putter out of the tree, officer," I replied.

"I'll give you one go at it. If you miss, that's it. Y'heah?"

Mirabile dictu, Dave shot the putter in one and down she came. Believe it or not, my putter was in no worse condition

Tony Costello in full flow, one of the finest ball strikers I ever saw.

after its hair-raising experience than any of the several hundred mangled, battered, ruined flat sticks that are hanging from the ceiling in the Davis garage—distorted and condemned, never to be used again.

"Serves 'em right for underperforming," I can hear Dave say between his teeth. All those once-beautiful, pristine putters had been brutalized to such an extent by his summary and ham-fisted "surgery" that none of them has ever been taken out onto a green again. In a magnanimous moment, Dave invited me to rescue from "death row"— and bring back to Ireland with me—any or as many of his putters as I wished. After carefully inspecting each and every one of them, I declined, much to the delight of his long-suffering wife. Fran Davis's long-held assertion that her husband was an abusive putterphile, and that "all of that ugly junk" should be thrown out with the garbage, was vindicated at last by somebody who knew his putters.

The reason for my occasional anger in public was the extreme frustration I felt toward myself for any less than satisfactory performances. I was conceited enough to think I could play perfect golf and would not tolerate anything less. This did not show much intelligence. My failure to win a major amateur championship was not because I was not good enough but because I got myself too worked up about it and tried too hard. I allowed minor setbacks to upset my focus and concentration. I was always peaking too soon, playing my best in practice and in the early rounds of championships, only to run out of steam before the week was over. I could reach great heights and then play tamely in the next round. It was Sam Snead who said he always wanted to play the guy who had played his best the day before because the chances of doing it two days in a row were slim. It would have been better if I could have sneaked up on the opposition by playing my way into top form, but I never had enough confidence and control. I always had to go flat-out from the beginning. That is fine in a sprint, but championships are marathons. You have to be able to control *yourself* as well as the ball.

When John Burke passed away in 1974, I suffered withdrawal symptoms until I found a pair of like-minded soul mates with whom I could join forces in the futile search for golfing nirvana. They were Derry Culligan and the late Tony Costello. Like golfing Musketeers, we spent hours poring over a book called *The Search for the Perfect Swing* by Alistair Cochran and John Stobbs. We rigged up a net, mats, and mirrors in Costello's basement on Barrington Street. I do not think it did us any harm, but neither did it do much good. We would have been far better off studying a book by psychologist Bob Rotella called *Golf Is Not A Game Of Perfect*. Unfortunately, this fascinating insight into

the golfing mind came too late because it was only published in 1995 and we were well past our best by then.

Without ever quite setting the world on fire, Costello
and Culligan were competitors of some note and highly
regarded and admired for their pure ball striking. But like
me, they underachieved. After one unexpectedly early exit
from the South of Ireland Championship at Lahinch, my
two friends "went missing." They did not even tell their wives
where they were going. They simply disappeared. When
neither came home that night, their wives compared notes
and became slightly worried. The next morning, the overdue phone call came:

"I am in London, dear."

"What are you doing in London? I thought you were in
Lahinch."

"We decided to come over to see Bill Cox (the premier
golf coach in England at the time). We were so disappointed with our play at Lahinch that we had to talk to him.
We'll be home tomorrow."

Cox said that Tony Costello was one of the finest strikers
of a golf ball he ever saw. He was a natural who really did not
need lessons, but the search for "perfection" never stopped.

One bitterly cold winter's day, Culligan and I were flog-
ging balls in splendid isolation on the Castle Course at
Lahinch. Immaculate 3-iron shots were being shelled out,
quail high, into a "black" wind. Both of us were "on song,"
and I could not help remarking, "Damn it, this is better
than sex!"

I will not tell you Derry's reply.

Culligan did not have Costello's natural power or my
flair with the putter, but he was the leader of the pack in
discovering ways to analyse the golf swing. He was the first
person I came across who advocated contrary repetitive
drills as a means of introducing a swing change. The only
problem was, should we have been changing our swings at all?

Derry Culligan was absolutely correct when he insisted
that as soon as anything started to go wrong with our games

the first thing to check out was setup and ball position. The majority of mistakes are determined before the club even moves. He maintained the swing itself was a fairly natural movement—influenced to a great degree by the size and shape of your body—and should largely be left alone

I suppose it was inevitable that no less a student of the golf swing than Nick Faldo (shortly before he met David Leadbetter), should have come in contact with Guru Culligan. It happened at a dinner party in Dublin during the Irish Open. The two of them ended up in the garden engaged in an intensive discussion on swing plane. Shortly afterward, Faldo became a major success. Erroneously, in my view, Leadbetter got the credit!

Having been exposed to all of this high-powered study of the game, what have I learned that might usefully be passed on to another generation of golf nuts?

"Keep it simple, stupid!"

Stick to the basics of good grip, good posture, proper aiming, and alignment, and let matters follow their own natural course. Swing the club straight back and straight through, with as much speed as you can muster. That is all there is to it. Your swing is your swing—right from the word go, from the time when you first took a club in your hands. You can build up strength and timing from practice, but the basic shape and plane of the swing is dictated by body shape and body type. You cannot change that. It is the mind and the way it works that separates us from mediocrity. If a young fellow asks me how he can improve, I simply tell him, "Hit the ball pure, try to control the clubhead, work on your short game, and compete as often as possible in as many different places and tournaments as you can."

When competing, adopt the trusty old adage of playing one shot at a time. This is easier said than done, but it works. I believe I was a particularly good foursomes player (alternate shot) because the format helped me to isolate each shot.

A few years ago, my own golf was in a complete shambles

because I had made the game too complicated. It was only when I managed to exorcise the demons in my head and got back to the basics that I began the slow recovery to acceptable golfing health. This had as much to do with the way I thought about things and approached the game as anything else.

The better the player, the more important the mental input needs to be. There has always been too much concentration on the technical side of golf and not enough on behaviour and self-management. I do not know of any other game that requires as much mental application. Golf is a static game. There is too much time to think. Conditions can change from day to day. Momentum can be turned upside down by one single shot. Golfers who analyse their swings in the middle of a game have no chance. They are only inviting killer tension, which destroys the best of swings.

⊛

CHAPTER 19

Back to the Future

Any notion that the golfers of yore were better than their present-day counterparts is nonsense. The human species is growing bigger, stronger, faster, and more knowledgeable all the time and it is bound to be all the better for it, not to mention the improvements in golf equipment. Twenty-first century golfers will be better in every way than the golfers who have gone before, and there will be more of them, making the competition tougher than ever. In every era, it has taken someone special to be a champion, and it will not be getting any easier.

That may be the reason why in the future there will be more and more reliance on dieticians, personal trainers, and sports therapists (physical *and* mental) by those with designs on the top. What goes on between the ears may be invisible, but it frequently dictates the difference between being a champion and an also-ran. The knowledge that we golfers have gained over the years will continue to be cultivated and passed on to future generations in a manner that, unfortunately, was not available to my generation.

Since I began playing there have been massive changes in the way the golf club is swung. The predominant use of hands and lots of moving parts in a flailing action has given way to shorter, tighter actions. Top players these days pull the club down toward the ball instead of "throwing" it at it. Fred Couples is one of the few who still throws the club into impact. There is much less leg movement than there used to be, as a solid lower body is needed to allow the arms to be kept closer together and more tightly connected to the body, with the big muscles of the back and shoulders supplying the power. Wrists are held firmer and swings are slower, particularly in the short game. The greater distances that modern players hit the ball is clearly helped by improvements in ball construction and science age materials in clubs, like titanium. Plus, the players are bigger, stronger, and fitter.

Thanks to the video camera, there has been an enormous improvement in coaching expertise. To be able to see yourself in action on a split screen beside a top performer is illuminating and vastly educational. If I could have had the luxury of that forty years ago, it would have speeded up my learning process. The short game is the area where the current players have improved the most. Sand play seems to have been mastered by everybody, and the conditions of greens and putting skills are hugely improved. To think that players sometimes play into bunkers *intentionally* these days is unbelievable in the context of the game as I once knew it. It makes me think that perhaps the time has come for rakes to be banned in order to bring some unpredictability back into bunker play. After all, hitting into a bunker is supposed to be a punishment for a poor shot—not a reward.

New ways of playing shots are being invented all the time. I wish that I had known about the bellied wedge or fairway wood chip forty years ago. I believe they would have saved me more than a few vital strokes. But easily the biggest change is not titanium metal heads, or triplex grass mowing equipment, or even the ball itself, but the huge increase in the number of people playing the game, resulting in uncomfortable, overcrowded courses everywhere. I find this hard to live with, and it is the one thing that could induce me to retire for good if it continues to grow unchecked. The only solution is to build more golf courses. When I began playing, we used the smaller (1.62 inch) ball. It was highly unpredictable and quite capable of diving violently. Amazingly—you would think it would be just the opposite—today's bigger ball (1.68 inch) is not affected by the wind as much as the smaller ball was. Modern science took care of that, thanks to such inventions as the wind tunnel and the various aerodynamic dimple arrangements on the ball's surface. Today's ball flies straighter and farther than its predecessors. Believe it or not, it was only in 1990 that the R&A wrote the 1.68 inch ball into the rules as statutory in Britain and Ireland. I spent my entire serious competitive career using the small ball. It was faster in the air and on the ground, which made it much more difficult to control. Around the green, it was practically impossible to stop. When the big ball arrived, older players like myself had to alter their techniques. Our active hand actions had to be curbed. Everything had to be firmed up to allow the big muscles to dictate as the hands became passive.

Modern golf balls are things of wonder and confusion. There are so many different types: Balata, Surlyn, Elastomer, to name just three cover constructions. They come in one, two, three, even four pieces. High- and low-trajectory. High- and low-spin. Distance. Distance? Would you believe a ball that goes farther! Now who in heaven's name would want that? The high-spin balata ball is a major asset to the skilful player. It allows more airborne golf instead of unpredictable along-the-ground stuff. And the useful skill of stopping a ball dead in its tracks became a lot easier when the balata ball was mass-produced.

Golf balls are now extremely consistent in their performance, which is a far cry from the time when rogue balls were common. There was a bit of a cover-up of an incident during the Jeyes Pro–Am Tournament at Killarney in 1966, for reasons that will be obvious. After thirty or so players had failed to get off the tee successfully by clearing 170 yards of swampy ground with the complimentary balls given to them by the Official Starter, it was decided to call the whole thing off and start all over again. After a single strike the balls had turned egg-shaped and would not fly.

Changing from the small ball to the big ball was a huge factor in narrowing the success deficit between American and European golfers. Until a standard ball was adopted, foreigners could not compete evenly with the Americans, especially on their home turf, and we were clobbered time after time in the Walker and Ryder Cups. I learned to play by *forcing* the small ball to do things, and I had a tough time adjusting to the big ball, whose built-in instinct was to fly higher and straighter.

I once had the opportunity to ask Gary Player what he thought was the biggest change in golf since he won the U.S. Open in 1965. Without hesitation, he said, "The ball." Gary does not have to fight for a place on crowded golf courses like I do, but looking at things from his perspective, he is correct, of course. The ball is so lively now that it is getting to the stage where only courses measuring over 7,500 yards will be considered suitable for professional tournaments. Today's golf courses are longer and more difficult than ever before, yet scores of twenty under par are frequent over 72 holes in professional events.

The improvement in golf course conditioning is a great source of pleasure to "old war horses" like myself. When I complain about a course's condition, it is because things are not as good as they could be rather than worse than they used to be. Golf courses are prepared for play in more sophisticated ways than ever. But they need to be, with all of the extra play on them. While all of the improvements have made golf courses greener and more beautiful to look at, they have also made them softer, slower, and muddier, and more likely to hold water. Once upon a time, it was highly unusual for a golf course to be closed for play. Perhaps the smaller numbers playing meant no harm would have been done if play were allowed to take place in inclement weather. These days courses are crowded from dawn until dusk, seven days a week, all year round, every-where you go. If ever they are declared unplayable, the numbers itching to get out often will have a big influence on the decision. All those golfers would destroy a course if let loose in unfavourable conditions.

Appearance-wise, the change in equipment has been remarkable. But apart from the titanium metal "wood," the advances in this area have had less impact than the manu-facturers would have us believe. Titanium seems to provide a kind of springboard flexibility to the clubface that increases the velocity of the ball coming off it. This explains one of the reasons why the ball is going farther and farther. I think we should try harder to maintain some semblance of the traditional way the game was played.

A man named Walter Pedersen must feel really hard done by as he watches modern golf from the bleachers in the sky. Walter invented aluminium-headed "woods" back in the 1920s, but the legislators of golf banned them. Pedersen's clubs were restricted to being used "for hire" at driving ranges only, because they stood up to abuse better than per-simmon. Walter called his clubs "Silver Knights." If he were alive in today's litigious world, I am sure he would be able to sue the R&A and USGA for millions of dollars and could have kept his descendants in untold wealth for generations.

For all of the many changes in the playing of the game, power is still the most important thing. To be able to hit a long ball has always been critical for anyone wanting to compete at the highest level. All parts of the game can be equalized except for raw power and the invisible mental side. Tiger Woods may have highlighted this state of affairs in a more spectacular fashion than ever before, but it has always been the case. Being on the fairway, being able to hit greens, being able to get up and down from off the green and out of hazards, and being able to putt can be taken for granted. Being able to hit the ball over three hundred yards cannot. That is a gift of nature, and it is what separates the guys at the pinnacle from the others. In my opinion, to tell youngsters that accuracy is more important than distance is hogwash. Every kid should first learn to hit the ball as far as he can and worry about control later. You can learn control; you cannot learn to hit the ball a mile. Golf is a power game: There is no better piece of equipment in your "arsenal" than the ability to hit a golf ball a long distance. When that gift is matched with the mind of a Jones, a Nicklaus, or a Woods, you've got a champion. In that sense, perhaps things have not changed at all.

❀

CHAPTER 20

Growing Old with Attitude
Senior Golf

With sincere apologies to Prince Hamlet of Denmark, I wish to end with a little rhyme concocted by, as far as I know, Eric Shaw, the youngest son of Sir Alec Shaw, the founding father of golf in Limerick and Lahinch, presumably for one of his Captain's Dinner speeches.

"To Be Or Not To Be"
I'd rather be a "Could Be,"
If I cannot be an "Are."
For a "Could Be" is a "Maybe,"
With a chance of beating par.
I'd rather be a "Has Been,"
Than a "Might Have Been" by far.
For a "Might Be" is a "Hasn't Been,"
But a "Has" was once an "Are."

I do not know much about growing old yet, but I do hope to have the privilege. There is at least one positive aspect to it and that is that it sure as hell beats the alternative. At age fifty-four I am foolishly wishing my life away so that I can get into Senior tournament golf and begin competing again. Deep down I must be an adrenaline junkie. Winning is not the ultimate purpose, although it would be nice, but the tingly feeling of being in the hunt certainly is. Casual golf is all very well, but there is no edge to it. I believe too much casual golf may be partly responsible for my increasingly scattered and disjointed performances. For too long I have been lacking in focus and without attainable goals. Without the self-imposed pressure of targets, I slipped into a grievous and disastrous occasion of "sin"—that is, playing a game called "Swing." Without competitive pressures I began trying to perfect my swing instead of concentrating on score, and only score, as I used to do. I have also missed competing because of the "buzz" one gets when things are going well. For me, golf between the ages of forty and fifty-five has been a limbo. It is far too long to be out of contention. I have been warned that Senior golf is completely different from normal tournament golf insofar as there is a drug test after every round, and anyone who is *not* on some substance or other is automatically disqualified. I do not know how I will cope with that situation, unless my eye-drops count as a chemical.

I am fascinated by the players on the U.S. Senior Tour who relish a second chance at a career that in many cases eluded them when they passed the age of forty. I also find it delightful when former journeymen professionals like Bruce Fleischer, Doug Tewell, and Dave Eichelberger—all of whom struggled for most of their golfing lives—achieve success beyond their wildest dreams in the Senior grade. How marvellous life can be if you keep trying and believe in yourself. Not many sportsmen are given a second chance of success past the age of fifty, but professional golfers are, and they relish it. When career amateurs like Jay Sigel, Allen Doyle, John Grace, and Denis O'Sullivan take a late plunge into the paid ranks and find the pot of gold, I am thrilled for them.

There is a hugely significant difference between amateur and professional golf at the Senior level. It is the age limit for qualification—50 for professionals and 55 for amateurs.

Why this should be does not make a lot of sense. Most top class amateurs these days are finished with competitive golf by the time they reach thirty years of age, as the demands of family and career prevent them from being able to give the time and commitment that is needed to play the game at the highest levels. That leaves too many years of waiting around for Senior golf to come along and provide the opportunity of winning something significant once more. This situation definitely needs to be addressed by the ruling bodies of amateur golf. One way to reduce the hardship is for more mid-amateur events for low-handicap amateurs to be arranged in order to fill the gap.

It was always in the back of my mind that I might like to try the Senior Professional Tour at the appropriate time. Unfortunately, when I reached the magic five-o my game was in tatters and I had a tough job breaking 75 consistently. There was no point in even thinking about trying my luck at playing for money. My amateur career lasted longer than most because I was pretty focussed and dedicated. I was also lucky that I had my own business, which allowed me the freedom to give the game more time than most people are able to give. Upon reaching the age of forty-five, I finally quit championship golf for good because I had lost my appetite and desire and my game had left me. I presume the two were connected, but I honestly think that a lack of focus and incentive was the critical factor.

When I began trying to rediscover my game, I quickly became sure of one thing: Focussing on a target, be it on the golf course or in the mind (ambition), is much more difficult as a fifty-four-year-old than it ever was as a twenty-year-old. I am beginning to wonder if I will ever get it back. The simple exercise of being able to look at the target and "see" the shot before starting the swing has become frustratingly elusive.

Those ten long years in the doldrums, however, taught me something else: My life was dull and incomplete without competitive golf. I am determined to press on, determined

Stay "slan" (healthy), and come to Ireland for some great golf.

to be in shape, ready for action, at age 55.

It is obvious that as we get older we lose physical skills that we once took for granted. But if we make allowances and utilize the mental skills acquired through experience, the drop-off in standards can be minimized. Older golfers readily tell me how age affects their play. Most say the first thing to go is the legs, then the ability to concentrate, as the hunger for victory wanes. Some say the nerves go, too, especially on the putting green. Any falloff in my putting is due to poor eyesight. I simply cannot see the lines as clearly as I used to, and the wearing of spectacles is an uncomfortable and not very effective necessity.

I have always been an above-average putter, but I am concerned that I might not be able to get my Tiger-like focus on the greens back when I need to. I was very interested in Tiger's comments to the media after his victory in the 2000 PGA Championship. He was asked how he managed to sink so many critical putts. He one-putted 11 of the last 15 greens.

"I think it is the product of a lot of hard work. I do not know if you can will the ball into the hole, but when I look back on those putts I realize that I was releasing the blade better than normally and (probably) because I am not thinking about it. I am just thinking about the hole and how I am going to get the ball in there."

That says it all for me as far as golf is concerned. On the practice tee you practice as much as you can to make the swing movements automatic. But when you are competing, you must think only of the target and of how to get the ball in the hole in as few shots as possible.

The inevitable loss of coordination, balance, and flexibility due to getting older impedes us all. So in order to combat these shortcomings I have taken to exercising and swinging a heavy club again. I have also found a therapist with "magic hands" who has helped to banish many of the old deep-rooted strains, sprains, and muscle injuries that were restricting me and holding me back. To keep the legs fit for action, I walk as much as I can, on and off the course. Because older players are not as flexible and cannot turn like the younger ones, it is imperative that the swing remains as long and as wide as possible into old age. That requires some strength and physical fitness. Short, narrow swings expedite a golfer's demise. A long, slow, wide swing has the added bonus of allowing more time for everything to get into position for the downswing attack on the ball.

It seems to me that golfers who were never low handicap players enjoy their golf far more in their advancing years. Having to accept less distance, fatter shots, and a decreased return on the greens leaves many former high-quality players frustrated and they give up. I am hoping that going to the gym, swinging a heavy club, and lots of walking and stretching will help me to keep going, otherwise I am going to have to take up knitting. It is too late to go back to hockey, rugby, or soccer. I hope to be able to conquer the weaknesses of the flesh with a willing spirit.

I learned a long time ago that golf is a game of minimizing mistakes. If we are to achieve anything in this life it must be to learn from one's mistakes. The older one becomes, the more mistakes one will have made, and hopefully the more one will have learned how to overcome them. Now *that* gives the old guys an advantage over the young fellows. One thing is for sure: I want to play as well as I can for as long as I can, and "Harrumph the begrudgers!"

I have dreamed many dreams that never came true.
I have seen them vanish at dawn.
I have realized enough of my dreams, thank God,
To make me want to dream on.
I have drained the cup of disappointment and pain
And gone many a day without song,
But I've sipped enough nectar from the roses of life
To make me want to live on.